Loving Christ Through St Josemaría Escrivá

Written by Holly Melita Teresa Rodriguez
Homilies and Reflections by St Josemaría Escrivá

Dedicated to Our Lady, The Mystic Rose
Ave Maria.

A Prayer before a Crucifix

Behold, O kind and most sweet Jesus,
I cast myself upon my knees in Thy sight, and with the most fervent
desire of my soul I pray and beseech Thee to impress upon my heart
lively sentiments of faith, hope and charity, with true repentance for
my sins and a most firm desire of amendment. Whilst with deep
affection and grief of soul I consider within myself and mentally
contemplate Thy five most precious wounds, having before my eyes
that which David, the prophet, long ago spoke concerning Thee,
"They have pierced My hands and My feet,
they have numbered all My bones."

A Plenary Indulgence applicable to the souls in purgatory may be
gained by all the faithful who after having confessed their sins with
true contrition, received the Blessed Sacrament and prayed for the
intentions of the Holy Father, Our Sovereign Pontiff, and devoutly
recite this prayer before an image or representation of
Christ Crucified.

"Love our Lady, and she will obtain abundant grace to help you conquer in your daily struggle."

- St Josemaría Escrivá.

Introduction

I wrote this book over the course of forty days from Christmas until Candlemas during the year 2020. The writings within these pages are from my personal diary as I journeyed for forty days in the desert with Our Lord, Jesus Christ in prayer and contemplation. Within these pages you will find reflections by St Josemaría Escrivá for each daily intention, along with prayers I've written and sacred scripture to contemplate on. Each day is devoted to Our lady through the Holy Rosary, as a way to grow closer to Christ through the guidance of St Josemaría Escrivá. I hope that you will find spiritual growth and a strengthened prayer life through these exercises. There is a consecration prayer at the end of the journey, which I have written for those who wish to consecrate themselves to St Josemaría Escrivá and adopt him as a companion for spiritual guidance and intercession. Each one of us has a unique journey with Christ, we will face many trials and many a 'dark night of the soul' through-out our Christian life. What is important is that we never give up, and to continue through these dark nights with Christ as our lantern to illuminate the path ahead which is unknown to us. We must persevere if we are to become saints, just as Christ himself persevered under the heavy weight of The Cross on the Via Dolorosa. This book is meant to help you persevere on that narrow path and remind you that you are never alone on that journey. You will always find comfort knowing that Christ and the saints are there with you, to help you up should you fall and to guide you ever closer to Christ through their intercession. Do not be afraid to call out to heaven for Our Lady and her intercession. She is a mother above all else, and what do mother's do best but to comfort and guide their children, keeping them safe from harm. Lean on her when you are feeling lost, she is the Morning Star that lights up the sky and acts as a compass on our journey to Christ. May God bless you and Our Lady shelter you in her most loving mantle.

Our Lady as Mediatrix

"I would recommend that, if you haven't already done so, you find out for yourself by personal experience the meaning of Mary's maternal love. It is not enough just to know she is our Mother and to think and to talk about her as such. She is your Mother. She loves you as if you were her only child in this world. Treat her accordingly: tell her about everything that happens to you, honour her and love her. No one will do it for you or as well as you, if you do not do it yourself. I give you my word that, if you set out along this way, you will quickly discover all the love of Christ: and you will find yourself drawn into the ineffable life of God the Father,
God the Son and God the Holy Spirit.

You will draw strength from it to put the Will of God fully into practice, and you will be filled with desires of serving all men. You will be the Christian you have sometimes dreamed of being: full of works of charity and justice, happy and strong, understanding towards others and demanding on yourself. This, and no other, is the kind of faith we want. Let us have recourse to our Mother Mary; she will accompany us and help us make firm and constant progress."

- St Josemaría Escrivá.

Dear Lord Jesus Christ, I humbly ask that You pardon me for my sins. I come to You as Your faithful servant, pleading with a true heart. Most precious and ever merciful Jesus Christ.

As I look at The Cross without the image of Christ, I know The Cross is for me. The only way is Your way, which is the way of The Cross. I will endure the heavy weight of The Cross because I love You, most precious Jesus.

I ask that You give me the strength to devote each day to You. Dear Lord, who suffered and was crucified because You love me. Thank You for all that You have given to me and to the world.

Amen.

Day One: A Peaceful Heart.

"What takes away your peace of soul cannot come from God. A clear mark of the man of God, of the woman of God, is the peace in their souls: they have peace, and they give peace to the people they have dealings with. We must bring people together, we must understand others, we must make allowances. Never put-up a cross just to keep alive the memory that some people have killed others. Such a cross would betoken the devil. Christ's cross is to keep silent, to forgive and to pray for those on both sides, so that all may attain peace. Just as Christ "went about doing good" throughout Palestine, so must you also spread peace in your family circle, in civil society, on the job, and in your cultural and leisure activities."

-St Josemaría Escrivá

Prayer Intention

Lord Jesus Christ, I desire to have a heart so full of love and burning with the same passion towards mankind as Your most Sacred Heart. I know that I cannot obtain a heart overflowing with Your peace and love so long as it harbours resentment and bitterness due to the wounds inflicted upon me.

"Let the peace of Christ be the controlling factor in your hearts. To this peace indeed you were called as members in one body and be thankful. Let the word of Christ richly dwell within you, with all wisdom teaching and admonishing one another with psalms and hymns and spiritual songs, singing with thankfulness in your hearts to God."

- Colossians 3:15-16

Day One: A Peaceful Heart.

Dear Lord, I humbly beg You, through the intercession of St Josemaría Escrivá for the grace of forgiveness and loving my enemies. I ask that You mend the deep wound which has become infected with the diseases of anger, bitterness, resentment, and malice. Please, Lord Jesus Christ who was crucified and risen, who has gifted me, a lowly sinner with Your infinite mercy and love, to bestow upon me a heart like Yours so that I may not trespass against others and so I may forgive those who have trespassed against me.

Prayer to St Josemaría Escrivá

Most loving God, through the mediation of Our Lady, the Blessed Virgin, You chose St Josemaría Escrivá to serve You and honour you. You have gifted St Josemaría Escrivá the wisdom and grace to form Opus Dei, a way of sanctification in daily work and in the fulfilment of the Christian's ordinary life and duties. Grant that I too may learn to turn my everyday life into one that serves You God, and imitates the way of St Josemaría Escrivá with a zeal for loving all souls and striving for sanctification. Grant unto me God, through the intercession of St Josemaría Escrivá the favour of (intention).

Day One: A Peaceful Heart.

"Now may the Lord of peace himself give you peace at all times and in every way. The Lord be with all of you."

- 2 Thessalonians 3:16

Holy Rosary of Joyful Mysteries

I believe in God, the Father Almighty, Creator of Heaven, and earth; and in Jesus Christ, His only Son, Our Lord, who was conceived by the Holy Ghost, born of the Virgin Mary, suffered under Pontius Pilate, was crucified; died, and was buried. He descended into Hell; the third day He arose again from the dead; He ascended into Heaven, sitteth at the right hand of God, the Father Almighty; from thence He shall come to judge the living and the dead. I believe in the Holy Spirit, the holy Catholic Church, the communion of saints, the forgiveness of sins, the resurrection of the body, and life everlasting.

Our Father, who art in heaven, hallowed be Thy name; Thy kingdom come; Thy will be done on earth as it is in heaven. Give us this day our daily bread; and forgive us our trespasses as we forgive those who trespass against us; and lead us not into temptation, but deliver us from evil.

Hail Mary, full of grace. The Lord is with thee. Blessed art thou among women, and blessed is the fruit of thy womb, Jesus. Holy Mary, Mother of God, pray for us sinners, now and at the hour of our death.

Glory be to the Father, to the Son, and to the Holy Spirit, as it was, is now, and ever shall be, world without end. Amen.

The Five Joyful Mysteries are prayed Monday and Saturday.

The Joyful Mysteries remind the faithful of Our Lady's Fiat and Christ's birth:

The Annunciation (Luke 1:26–38); The Visitation (Luke 1:39–56) The Nativity (Luke 2:1–21); The Presentation (Luke 2:22–38) The Finding of the Child Jesus in the Temple (Luke 2:41–52)

Hail Holy Queen

Hail, Holy Queen, Mother of mercy, our life, our sweetness, and our hope. To thee do we cry, poor banished children of Eve, to thee do we send up our sighs, mourning and weeping in this vale of tears. Turn then, most gracious advocate, thine eyes of mercy toward us; and after this our exile show unto us the blessed fruit of thy womb Jesus, O clement, O loving, O sweet Virgin Mary.

Pray for us, O holy Mother of God. That we may be made worthy of the promises of Christ.

O God, whose only begotten Son, by His life, death, and resurrection, has purchased for us the rewards of eternal salvation; grant we beseech Thee, that meditating upon these mysteries of the most holy Rosary of the Blessed Virgin Mary, we may imitate what they contain and obtain what they promise, through the same Christ our Lord.

Prayer to Our Lady of Guadalupe

Our Lady of Guadalupe, Mystical Rose, make intercession for the Holy Church, protect the Sovereign Pontiff, help all those who invoke thee in their necessities, and since thou art the Blessed Virgin Mary, and Mother of the True God, obtain for us from thy most holy Son the grace of keeping our faith, of sweet hope in the midst of the bitterness of life, of burning charity, and the most precious gift of perseverance so that we may carry our cross cheerfully.

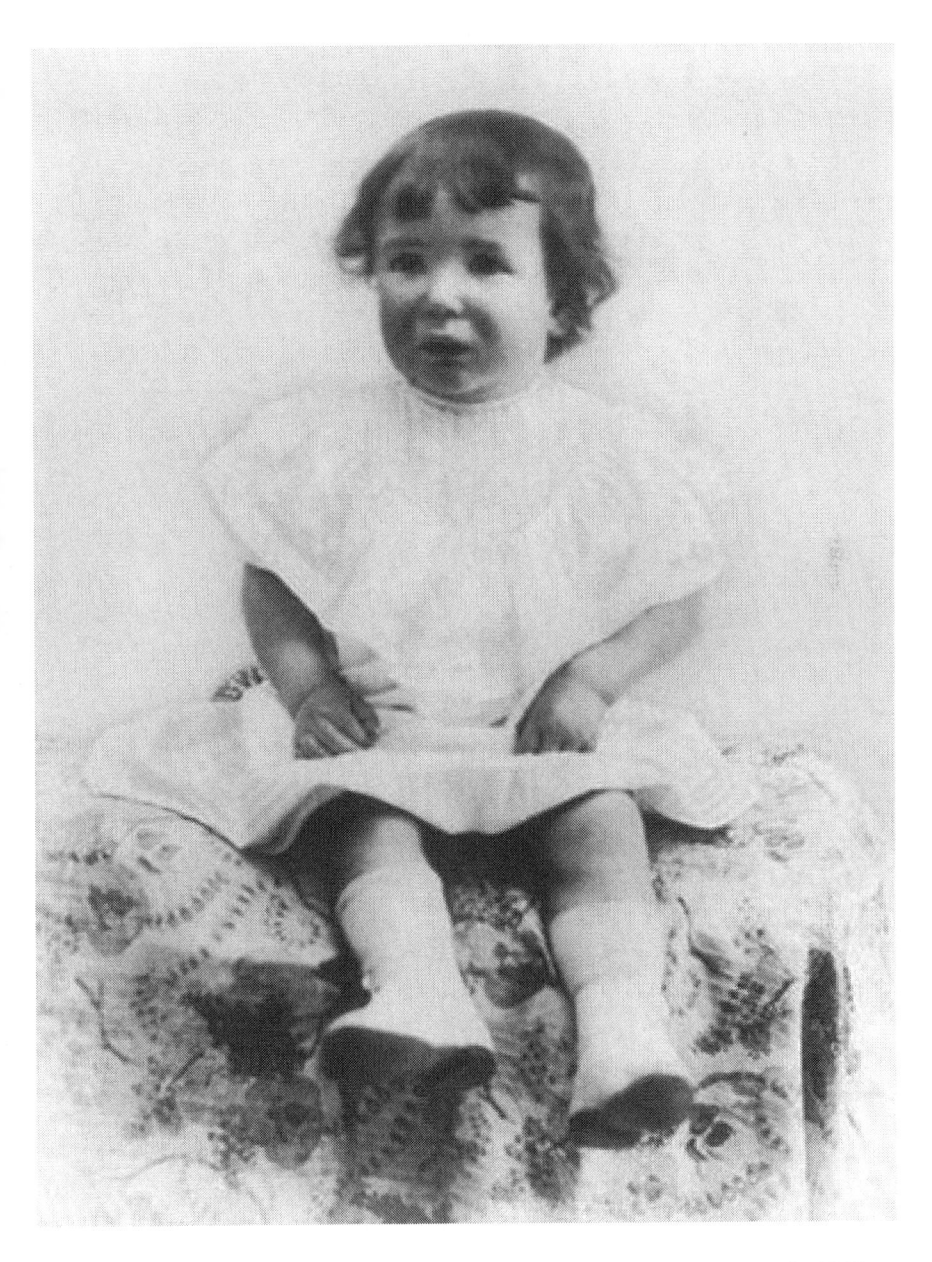

St Josemaría Escrivá was born in Barbastro, Spain on January 9, 1902.

Day Two: The Christian Family.

"When I think of Christian homes, I like to imagine them as being full of the light and joy that were in the home of the Holy Family. The message of Christmas is heard in all its forcefulness: 'Glory to God in the highest, and on earth peace to men of good will.' 'And may the peace of Christ triumph in your hearts,' writes the Apostle. It is a peace that comes from knowing that our Father God loves us, and that we are made one with Christ. It results from being under the protection of the Virgin, Our Lady, and assisted by St Joseph.

This is the great light that illuminates our lives. In the midst of difficulties and of our own personal failings, it encourages us to keep up our effort. Every Christian home should be a place of peace and serenity. In spite of the small frustrations of daily life, an atmosphere of profound and sincere affection should reign there together with a deep-rooted calm, which is the result of authentic faith that is put into practice."

-St Josemaría Escrivá

Prayer Intention

Lord Jesus Christ, I desire to make my home one of great devotion to You. Our family is a gift, and it is out of love that we lead one another toward sanctity in our daily lives. A family that imitates the Holy Family is one that is full of love, hope, and trust.

"Love is patient, love is kind. It does not envy, it does not boast, it is not proud. It does not dishonour others, it is not self- seeking, it is not easily angered, it keeps no record of wrongs. Love does not delight in evil but rejoices with the truth. It always protects, always trusts, always hopes, always perseveres. Love never fails."

- 1 Corinthians 13:4-8

Day Two: The Christian Family.

Dear Lord, I humbly beg You, through the intercession of St Josemaría Escrivá for the grace to overflow my heart with gratitude like Your most Sacred Heart, so that I may rejoice in my family and journey with them on the path toward heaven, helping them up when they should stumble. May they keep close to You Christ, and one day become Saints in the kingdom of heaven.

Prayer to St Josemaría Escrivá

Most loving God, through the mediation of Our Lady, the Blessed Virgin, You chose St Josemaría Escrivá to serve You and honour you. You have gifted St Josemaría Escrivá the wisdom and grace to form Opus Dei, a way of sanctification in daily work and in the fulfilment of the Christian's ordinary life and duties. Grant that I too may learn to turn my everyday life into one that serves You God, and imitates the way of St Josemaría Escrivá with a zeal for loving all souls and striving for sanctification. Grant unto me God, through the intercession of St Josemaría Escrivá the favour of (intention).

Day Two: The Christian Family.

"Answer me when I call, O God of my righteousness! You have given me relief when I was in distress. Be gracious to me, and hear my prayer!"

- Psalm 4:1

Holy Rosary of Sorrowful Mysteries

I believe in God, the Father Almighty, Creator of Heaven, and earth; and in Jesus Christ, His only Son, Our Lord, who was conceived by the Holy Ghost, born of the Virgin Mary, suffered under Pontius Pilate, was crucified; died, and was buried. He descended into Hell; the third day He arose again from the dead; He ascended into Heaven, sitteth at the right hand of God, the Father Almighty; from thence He shall come to judge the living and the dead. I believe in the Holy Spirit, the holy Catholic Church, the communion of saints, the forgiveness of sins, the resurrection of the body, and life everlasting.

Our Father, who art in heaven, hallowed be Thy name; Thy kingdom come; Thy will be done on earth as it is in heaven. Give us this day our daily bread; and forgive us our trespasses as we forgive those who trespass against us; and lead us not into temptation, but deliver us from evil.

Hail Mary, full of grace. The Lord is with thee. Blessed art thou among women, and blessed is the fruit of thy womb, Jesus. Holy Mary, Mother of God, pray for us sinners, now and at the hour of our death.

Glory be to the Father, to the Son, and to the Holy Spirit, as it was, is now, and ever shall be, world without end. Amen.

The Five Sorrowful Mysteries are prayed Tuesday and Friday.

The Sorrowful Mysteries remind the faithful of Christ's Passion and of His Crucifixion:

The Agony of Jesus in the Garden (Matthew 26:36–56); The Scourging at the Pillar (Matthew 27:26) The Crowning with Thorns (Matthew 27:27–31); The Carrying of the Cross (Matthew 27:32) The Crucifixion (Matthew 27:33–56)

Hail Holy Queen

Hail, Holy Queen, Mother of mercy, our life, our sweetness, and our hope. To thee do we cry, poor banished children of Eve, to thee do we send up our sighs, mourning and weeping in this vale of tears. Turn then, most gracious advocate, thine eyes of mercy toward us; and after this our exile show unto us the blessed fruit of thy womb Jesus, O clement, O loving, O sweet Virgin Mary.

Pray for us, O holy Mother of God. That we may be made worthy of the promises of Christ.

O God, whose only begotten Son, by His life, death, and resurrection, has purchased for us the rewards of eternal salvation; grant we beseech Thee, that meditating upon these mysteries of the most holy Rosary of the Blessed Virgin Mary, we may imitate what they contain and obtain what they promise, through the same Christ our Lord.

Prayer to Our Lady of Guadalupe

Our Lady of Guadalupe, Mystical Rose, make intercession for the Holy Church, protect the Sovereign Pontiff, help all those who invoke thee in their necessities, and since thou art the Blessed Virgin Mary, and Mother of the True God, obtain for us from thy most holy Son the grace of keeping our faith, of sweet hope in the midst of the bitterness of life, of burning charity, and the most precious gift of perseverance so that we may carry our cross cheerfully.

St Josemaría Escrivá in 1921.

Day Three: Charity.

"By living charity; love, you live all the human and supernatural virtues demanded of a Christian. These virtues form a unity and cannot be reduced to a mere list. You cannot have charity without justice, solidarity, family and social responsibility, poverty, joy, chastity, friendship...You can see immediately that the practice of these virtues leads to apostolate. In fact, it already is apostolate. For when people try to live in this way in the middle of their daily work, their Christian behaviour becomes a good example, witness, something which is a real and effective help to others."

-St Josemaría Escrivá

Prayer Intention

Lord Jesus Christ, I desire to be as loving and as charitable as You. Please soften my heart so that I can effectively love my neighbour and show the world what it means to be Your follower. Sweet Jesus Christ who was born in a manger so meek and mild and was crucified as an innocent man for the sake of love.

"If I speak in the tongues of men and of angels, but have not love, I am a noisy gong or a clanging cymbal. And if I have prophetic powers, and understand all mysteries and all knowledge, and if I have all faith, so as to remove mountains, but have not love, I am nothing. If I give away all I have, and if I deliver up my body to be burned, but have not love, I gain nothing. Love is patient and kind; love does not envy or boast; it is not arrogant or rude. It does not insist on its own way; it is not irritable or resentful."

- 1 Corinthians 13:1-13

Day Three: Charity.

Dear Lord, I humbly beg You, through the intercession of St Josemaría Escrivá, for the grace to be charitable in my thoughts, deeds, and prayers. I ask that You keep me focused on what I can do to serve You by serving others in charity, instead of being self-serving and only looking out for myself which is contrary to Your commandment of loving thy neighbour.

Prayer to St Josemaría Escrivá

Most loving God, through the mediation of Our Lady, the Blessed Virgin, You chose St Josemaría Escrivá to serve You and honour you. You have gifted St Josemaría Escrivá the wisdom and grace to form Opus Dei, a way of sanctification in daily work and in the fulfilment of the Christian's ordinary life and duties. Grant that I too may learn to turn my everyday life into one that serves You God, and imitates the way of St Josemaría Escrivá with a zeal for loving all souls and striving for sanctification. Grant unto me God, through the intercession of St Josemaría Escrivá the favour of (intention).

Day Three: Charity.

"Therefore, I tell you, whatever you ask in prayer, believe that you have received it, and it will be yours."

- Mark 11:24

Holy Rosary of Glorious Mysteries

I believe in God, the Father Almighty, Creator of Heaven, and earth; and in Jesus Christ, His only Son, Our Lord, who was conceived by the Holy Ghost, born of the Virgin Mary, suffered under Pontius Pilate, was crucified; died, and was buried. He descended into Hell; the third day He arose again from the dead; He ascended into Heaven, sitteth at the right hand of God, the Father Almighty; from thence He shall come to judge the living and the dead. I believe in the Holy Spirit, the holy Catholic Church, the communion of saints, the forgiveness of sins, the resurrection of the body, and life everlasting.

Our Father, who art in heaven, hallowed be Thy name; Thy kingdom come; Thy will be done on earth as it is in heaven. Give us this day our daily bread; and forgive us our trespasses as we forgive those who trespass against us; and lead us not into temptation, but deliver us from evil.

Hail Mary, full of grace. The Lord is with thee. Blessed art thou among women, and blessed is the fruit of thy womb, Jesus. Holy Mary, Mother of God, pray for us sinners, now and at the hour of our death.

Glory be to the Father, to the Son, and to the Holy Spirit, as it was, is now, and ever shall be, world without end. Amen.

The Five Glorious Mysteries are prayed Wednesday and Sunday.

The Glorious Mysteries remind the faithful of Christ's Resurrection and Heaven's glories:

The Resurrection (Luke 24:1-12); The Ascension (Acts 1:6-11) The Descent of the Holy Spirit (Acts 2:1-4); The Assumption (Munificentissimus Deus 44) The Coronation of Mary as Queen of Heaven (Revelations 12:1-6)

Hail Holy Queen

Hail, Holy Queen, Mother of mercy, our life, our sweetness, and our hope. To thee do we cry, poor banished children of Eve, to thee do we send up our sighs, mourning and weeping in this vale of tears. Turn then, most gracious advocate, thine eyes of mercy toward us; and after this our exile show unto us the blessed fruit of thy womb Jesus, O clement, O loving, O sweet Virgin Mary.

Pray for us, O holy Mother of God. That we may be made worthy of the promises of Christ.

O God, whose only begotten Son, by His life, death, and resurrection, has purchased for us the rewards of eternal salvation; grant we beseech Thee, that meditating upon these mysteries of the most holy Rosary of the Blessed Virgin Mary, we may imitate what they contain and obtain what they promise, through the same Christ our Lord.

Prayer to Our Lady of Guadalupe

Our Lady of Guadalupe, Mystical Rose, make intercession for the Holy Church, protect the Sovereign Pontiff, help all those who invoke thee in their necessities, and since thou art the Blessed Virgin Mary, and Mother of the True God, obtain for us from thy most holy Son the grace of keeping our faith, of sweet hope in the midst of the bitterness of life, of burning charity, and the most precious gift of perseverance so that we may carry our cross cheerfully.

St Josemaría Escrivá was an ambitious, bright and cheerful student.

Day Four: The Way of The Cross.

"Suffering overwhelms you because you take it like a coward. Meet it bravely, with a Christian spirit: and you will regard it as a treasure. Jesus suffers to carry out the will of the Father. And you, who also want to carry out the most holy Will of God, following the steps of the Master, can you complain if you meet suffering on your way?"

-St Josemaría Escrivá

Prayer Intention

Lord Jesus Christ, I desire to carry my cross without complaint as You did during the Crucifixion. Please give me the strength and courage of Your most precious Sacred Heart as I journey the Via Dolorosa with You in this Vale of tears, most loving Jesus Christ who suffered and was crucified for me.

"More than that, we rejoice in our sufferings, knowing that suffering produces endurance, and endurance produces character, and character produces hope, and hope does not put us to shame, because God's love has been poured into our hearts through the Holy Spirit who has been given to us. For while we were still helpless, at the right time Christ died for the ungodly. For one will hardly die for a righteous man; though perhaps for the good man someone would dare even to die. But God demonstrates His own love toward us, in that while we were yet sinners, Christ died for us."

- Romans 5:3-8

Day Four: The Way of The Cross.

Dear Lord, I humbly beg You, through the intercession of St Josemaría Escrivá, for the grace to suffer with You and endure my suffering with gratitude and cheerfulness. Please protect my heart from the wicked snares of the devil who would have me sow seeds of disharmony and bitterness over the suffering which is meant to sanctify me and bring me closer to You, most loving Christ.

Prayer to St Josemaría Escrivá

Most loving God, through the mediation of Our Lady, the Blessed Virgin, You chose St Josemaría Escrivá to serve You and honour you. You have gifted St Josemaría Escrivá the wisdom and grace to form Opus Dei, a way of sanctification in daily work and in the fulfilment of the Christian's ordinary life and duties. Grant that I too may learn to turn my everyday life into one that serves You God, and imitates the way of St Josemaría Escrivá with a zeal for loving all souls and striving for sanctification. Grant unto me God, through the intercession of St Josemaría Escrivá the favour of (intention).

Day Four: The Way of The Cross.

"For the preaching of the cross is to them that perish foolishness; but unto us which are saved it is the power of God."

- 1 Corinthians 1:18

Holy Rosary of Luminous Mysteries

I believe in God, the Father Almighty, Creator of Heaven, and earth; and in Jesus Christ, His only Son, Our Lord, who was conceived by the Holy Ghost, born of the Virgin Mary, suffered under Pontius Pilate, was crucified; died, and was buried. He descended into Hell; the third day He arose again from the dead; He ascended into Heaven, sitteth at the right hand of God, the Father Almighty; from thence He shall come to judge the living and the dead. I believe in the Holy Spirit, the holy Catholic Church, the communion of saints, the forgiveness of sins, the resurrection of the body, and life everlasting.

Our Father, who art in heaven, hallowed be Thy name; Thy kingdom come; Thy will be done on earth as it is in heaven. Give us this day our daily bread; and forgive us our trespasses as we forgive those who trespass against us; and lead us not into temptation, but deliver us from evil.

Hail Mary, full of grace. The Lord is with thee. Blessed art thou among women, and blessed is the fruit of thy womb, Jesus. Holy Mary, Mother of God, pray for us sinners, now and at the hour of our death.

Glory be to the Father, to the Son, and to the Holy Spirit, as it was, is now, and ever shall be, world without end. Amen.

The Five Luminous Mysteries are prayed on Thursday.

The Luminous Mysteries remind the faithful of Christ's shining light:

The Baptism in the River Jordan (Matthew 3:13–16); The Wedding Feast at Cana (John 2:1–11) The Preaching of the coming of the Kingdom of God (Mark 1:14–15) The Transfiguration (Matthew 17:1–8); The Institution of the Holy Eucharist (Matthew 26)

Hail Holy Queen

Hail, Holy Queen, Mother of mercy, our life, our sweetness, and our hope. To thee do we cry, poor banished children of Eve, to thee do we send up our sighs, mourning and weeping in this vale of tears. Turn then, most gracious advocate, thine eyes of mercy toward us; and after this our exile show unto us the blessed fruit of thy womb Jesus, O clement, O loving, O sweet Virgin Mary.

Pray for us, O holy Mother of God. That we may be made worthy of the promises of Christ.

O God, whose only begotten Son, by His life, death, and resurrection, has purchased for us the rewards of eternal salvation; grant we beseech Thee, that meditating upon these mysteries of the most holy Rosary of the Blessed Virgin Mary, we may imitate what they contain and obtain what they promise, through the same Christ our Lord.

Prayer to Our Lady of Guadalupe

Our Lady of Guadalupe, Mystical Rose, make intercession for the Holy Church, protect the Sovereign Pontiff, help all those who invoke thee in their necessities, and since thou art the Blessed Virgin Mary, and Mother of the True God, obtain for us from thy most holy Son the grace of keeping our faith, of sweet hope in the midst of the bitterness of life, of burning charity, and the most precious gift of perseverance so that we may carry our cross cheerfully.

St Josemaría Escrivá heard God's call to the priesthood at age sixteen.

Day Five: Dedication.

"It is utterly false to oppose freedom and self-surrender, because self-surrender is a consequence of freedom. Look, when a mother sacrifices herself for love of her children, she has made a choice, and the more she loves the greater will be her freedom. If her love is great, her freedom will bear much fruit. Her children's good derives from her blessed freedom, which presupposes self-surrender, and from her blessed self-surrender, which is precisely freedom."

-St Josemaría Escrivá

Prayer Intention

Lord Jesus Christ, I desire to dedicate my whole life to You and your will. I know that I cannot dedicate myself to You fully without the sacraments and daily prayer. Please use me to carry out Your will for the benefit of others and especially for serving Your bride, the holy apostolic Catholic Church. Lord I ask of You to give me a heart as dedicated to You as the heart of St Teresa of Avila, burning with passion for You.

"Blessed is the man who walks not in the counsel of the wicked, nor stands in the way of sinners, nor sits in the seat of scoffers; but his delight is in the law of the Lord, and on his law, he meditates day and night. He is like a tree planted by streams of water that yields its fruit in its season, and its leaf does not wither. In all that he does, he prospers. The wicked are not so but are like chaff that the wind drives away. Therefore, the wicked will not stand in the judgment, nor sinners in the congregation of the righteous."

- Psalms 1:1-6

Day Five: Dedication.

Dear Lord, I humbly beg You, through the intercession of St Josemaría Escrivá, for the grace to dedicate my work, my thoughts, and my whole being to your most holy will. I ask that You allow me to dedicate myself as much as Your holy priest St Josemaría Escrivá who founded Opus Dei did, and by Your grace, that I might also open my heart so that I can dedicate each day of my life, which is a gift, to You Lord, just as the saints in heaven serve You.

Prayer to St Josemaría Escrivá

Most loving God, through the mediation of Our Lady, the Blessed Virgin, You chose St Josemaría Escrivá to serve You and honour you. You have gifted St Josemaría Escrivá the wisdom and grace to form Opus Dei, a way of sanctification in daily work and in the fulfilment of the Christian's ordinary life and duties. Grant that I too may learn to turn my everyday life into one that serves You God, and imitates the way of St Josemaría Escrivá with a zeal for loving all souls and striving for sanctification. Grant unto me God, through the intercession of St Josemaría Escrivá the favour of (intention).

Day Five: Dedication.

"I am praying for them. I am not praying for the world but for those whom you have given me, for they are yours."

- John 17:9

Holy Rosary of Joyful Mysteries

I believe in God, the Father Almighty, Creator of Heaven, and earth; and in Jesus Christ, His only Son, Our Lord, who was conceived by the Holy Ghost, born of the Virgin Mary, suffered under Pontius Pilate, was crucified; died, and was buried. He descended into Hell; the third day He arose again from the dead; He ascended into Heaven, sitteth at the right hand of God, the Father Almighty; from thence He shall come to judge the living and the dead. I believe in the Holy Spirit, the holy Catholic Church, the communion of saints, the forgiveness of sins, the resurrection of the body, and life everlasting.

Our Father, who art in heaven, hallowed be Thy name; Thy kingdom come; Thy will be done on earth as it is in heaven. Give us this day our daily bread; and forgive us our trespasses as we forgive those who trespass against us; and lead us not into temptation, but deliver us from evil.

Hail Mary, full of grace. The Lord is with thee. Blessed art thou among women, and blessed is the fruit of thy womb, Jesus. Holy Mary, Mother of God, pray for us sinners, now and at the hour of our death.

Glory be to the Father, to the Son, and to the Holy Spirit, as it was, is now, and ever shall be, world without end. Amen.

The Five Joyful Mysteries are prayed Monday and Saturday.

The Joyful Mysteries remind the faithful of Our Lady's Fiat and Christ's birth:

The Annunciation (Luke 1:26–38); The Visitation (Luke 1:39–56) The Nativity (Luke 2:1–21); The Presentation (Luke 2:22–38) The Finding of the Child Jesus in the Temple (Luke 2:41–52)

Hail Holy Queen

Hail, Holy Queen, Mother of mercy, our life, our sweetness, and our hope. To thee do we cry, poor banished children of Eve, to thee do we send up our sighs, mourning and weeping in this vale of tears. Turn then, most gracious advocate, thine eyes of mercy toward us; and after this our exile show unto us the blessed fruit of thy womb Jesus, O clement, O loving, O sweet Virgin Mary.

Pray for us, O holy Mother of God. That we may be made worthy of the promises of Christ.

O God, whose only begotten Son, by His life, death, and resurrection, has purchased for us the rewards of eternal salvation; grant we beseech Thee, that meditating upon these mysteries of the most holy Rosary of the Blessed Virgin Mary, we may imitate what they contain and obtain what they promise, through the same Christ our Lord.

Prayer to Our Lady of Guadalupe

Our Lady of Guadalupe, Mystical Rose, make intercession for the Holy Church, protect the Sovereign Pontiff, help all those who invoke thee in their necessities, and since thou art the Blessed Virgin Mary, and Mother of the True God, obtain for us from thy most holy Son the grace of keeping our faith, of sweet hope in the midst of the bitterness of life, of burning charity, and the most precious gift of perseverance so that we may carry our cross cheerfully.

St Josemaría Escrivá at the Seminary of San Carlos in Zaragoza.

Day Six: Hope.

"In my case, and I wish the same to happen to you, the certainty I derive from feeling, from knowing that I am a son of God fills me with real hope which, being a supernatural virtue, adapts to our nature when it is infused in us, and so is also a very human virtue. I am happy because I am certain we will attain Heaven if we remain faithful to the end; I rejoice in the thought of the bliss that will be ours, quoniam bonus, because my God is good, and His mercy infinite."

-St Josemaría Escrivá

Prayer Intention

Lord Jesus Christ, I desire to have a hopeful spirit and never lose hope, even during times of great struggle and hardship. I know that I cannot persevere without Your guidance and without the intercession of the Saints and by regularly attending holy Mass. I must work hard to keep hope alive, not only in my own Christian heart but in the hearts of others, and I can do this by being Your witness and trusting in You, Lord Jesus Christ.

"After you have suffered for a little while, the God of all grace, the one who called you into his eternal glory in Christ Jesus, will himself restore, empower, strengthen, and establish you. To him is the glory and the dominion into the ages of the ages. Truly."

- 1 Peter 5:10-11

Day Six: Hope.

Dear Lord I humbly beg You, through the intercession of St Josemaría Escrivá, for the grace to start each day with a hopeful attitude. That I dedicate each and every day to Your most Holy Church and helping the Church to grow and foster hope in others through Your will in acts of love and charity. May I ask for no reward and find gratitude in each hope filled day that You have blessed me with life, so that I may use it to serve You.

Prayer to St Josemaría Escrivá

Most loving God, through the mediation of Our Lady, the Blessed Virgin, You chose St Josemaría Escrivá to serve You and honour you. You have gifted St Josemaría Escrivá the wisdom and grace to form Opus Dei, a way of sanctification in daily work and in the fulfilment of the Christian's ordinary life and duties. Grant that I too may learn to turn my everyday life into one that serves You God, and imitates the way of St Josemaría Escrivá with a zeal for loving all souls and striving for sanctification. Grant unto me God, through the intercession of St Josemaría Escrivá the favour of (intention).

Day Six: Hope.

Holy Rosary of Sorrowful Mysteries

*I believe in God, the Father Almighty, Creator of Heaven, and earth;
and in Jesus Christ, His only Son, Our Lord, who was conceived by
the Holy Ghost, born of the Virgin Mary, suffered under Pontius
Pilate, was crucified; died, and was buried. He descended into Hell;
the third day He arose again from the dead; He ascended into
Heaven, sitteth at the right hand of God, the Father Almighty; from
thence He shall come to judge the living and the dead. I believe in
the Holy Spirit, the holy Catholic Church, the communion of saints,
the forgiveness of sins, the resurrection of the body,
and life everlasting.*

*Our Father, who art in heaven, hallowed be Thy name; Thy kingdom
come; Thy will be done on earth as it is in heaven. Give us this day
our daily bread; and forgive us our trespasses as we forgive those
who trespass against us; and lead us not into temptation,
but deliver us from evil.*

*Hail Mary, full of grace. The Lord is with thee. Blessed art thou
among women, and blessed is the fruit of thy womb, Jesus. Holy
Mary, Mother of God, pray for us sinners,
now and at the hour of our death.*

Glory be to the Father, to the Son, and to the Holy Spirit, as it was, is now, and ever shall be, world without end. Amen.

The Five Sorrowful Mysteries are prayed Tuesday and Friday.

The Sorrowful Mysteries remind the faithful of Christ's Passion and of His Crucifixion:

The Agony of Jesus in the Garden (Matthew 26:36–56); The Scourging at the Pillar (Matthew 27:26) The Crowning with Thorns (Matthew 27:27–31); The Carrying of the Cross (Matthew 27:32) The Crucifixion (Matthew 27:33–56)

Hail Holy Queen

Hail, Holy Queen, Mother of mercy, our life, our sweetness, and our hope. To thee do we cry, poor banished children of Eve, to thee do we send up our sighs, mourning and weeping in this vale of tears. Turn then, most gracious advocate, thine eyes of mercy toward us; and after this our exile show unto us the blessed fruit of thy womb Jesus, O clement, O loving, O sweet Virgin Mary.

Pray for us, O holy Mother of God. That we may be made worthy of the promises of Christ.

O God, whose only begotten Son, by His life, death, and resurrection, has purchased for us the rewards of eternal salvation; grant we beseech Thee, that meditating upon these mysteries of the most holy Rosary of the Blessed Virgin Mary, we may imitate what they contain and obtain what they promise, through the same Christ our Lord.

Prayer to Our Lady of Guadalupe

Our Lady of Guadalupe, Mystical Rose, make intercession for the Holy Church, protect the Sovereign Pontiff, help all those who invoke thee in their necessities, and since thou art the Blessed Virgin Mary, and Mother of the True God, obtain for us from thy most holy Son the grace of keeping our faith, of sweet hope in the midst of the bitterness of life, of burning charity, and the most precious gift of perseverance so that we may carry our cross cheerfully.

St Josemaría Escrivá with his younger brother Santiago in Zaragoza, 1921.

Day Seven: Sainthood.

"We should not be surprised to find ourselves defeated relatively often, usually or even always in things of little importance which we tend to take seriously. If we love God and are humble, if we persevere relentlessly in our struggle, the defeats will never be very important. There will also be abundant victories which bring joy to God's eyes. There is no such thing as failure if you act with a right intention, wanting to fulfil God's will and counting always on His grace and your own nothingness."

-St Josemaría Escrivá

Prayer Intention

Lord Jesus Christ, I desire to walk with you down the path of sainthood. I know that on this path I will stumble and fall many times and face many struggles. I know that I cannot persevere on the path to sainthood without your guidance and without the sacraments. Lord Jesus Christ, I ask that you keep me on the straight and narrow path which leads through the gate of your kingdom. I will continue to dust myself off each time I fall, and I know that with your mercy, love, and protection that I will make it.

"Though youths grow weary and tired, and vigorous young men stumble badly, yet those who wait for the Lord will gain new strength; they will mount up with wings like eagles, they will run and not get tired, they will walk and not become weary."

- Isiah 40:30-31

Day Seven: Sainthood.

Dear Lord, I humbly beg you, through the intercession of St Josemaría Escrivá, for the grace to walk my path towards sainthood with fiery passion and zeal. Should I ever meet an occasion where I should stumble and fall into temptation or sin, that I will humble myself with the sacrament of confession so that I may continue on my journey, devoting my life to You Lord Jesus Christ.

Prayer to St Josemaría Escrivá

Most loving God, through the mediation of Our Lady, the Blessed Virgin, You chose St Josemaría Escrivá to serve You and honour you. You have gifted St Josemaría Escrivá the wisdom and grace to form Opus Dei, a way of sanctification in daily work and in the fulfilment of the Christian's ordinary life and duties. Grant that I too may learn to turn my everyday life into one that serves You God, and imitates the way of St Josemaría Escrivá with a zeal for loving all souls and striving for sanctification. Grant unto me God, through the intercession of St Josemaría Escrivá the favour of (intention).

Day Seven: Sainthood.

"Let your reasonableness be known to everyone. The Lord is at hand; do not be anxious about anything, but in everything by prayer and supplication with thanksgiving let your requests be made known to God. And the peace of God, which surpasses all understanding, will guard your hearts and your minds in Christ Jesus."

- Romans 12:12

Holy Rosary of Glorious Mysteries

I believe in God, the Father Almighty, Creator of Heaven, and earth; and in Jesus Christ, His only Son, Our Lord, who was conceived by the Holy Ghost, born of the Virgin Mary, suffered under Pontius Pilate, was crucified; died, and was buried. He descended into Hell; the third day He arose again from the dead; He ascended into Heaven, sitteth at the right hand of God, the Father Almighty; from thence He shall come to judge the living and the dead. I believe in the Holy Spirit, the holy Catholic Church, the communion of saints, the forgiveness of sins, the resurrection of the body, and life everlasting.

Our Father, who art in heaven, hallowed be Thy name; Thy kingdom come; Thy will be done on earth as it is in heaven. Give us this day our daily bread; and forgive us our trespasses as we forgive those who trespass against us; and lead us not into temptation, but deliver us from evil.

Hail Mary, full of grace. The Lord is with thee. Blessed art thou among women, and blessed is the fruit of thy womb, Jesus. Holy Mary, Mother of God, pray for us sinners, now and at the hour of our death.

Glory be to the Father, to the Son, and to the Holy Spirit, as it was, is now, and ever shall be, world without end. Amen.

The Five Glorious Mysteries are prayed Wednesday and Sunday.

The Glorious Mysteries remind the faithful of Christ's Resurrection and Heaven's glories:

The Resurrection (Luke 24:1-12); The Ascension (Acts 1:6-11) The Descent of the Holy Spirit (Acts 2:1-4); The Assumption (Munificentissimus Deus 44) The Coronation of Mary as Queen of Heaven (Revelations 12:1-6)

Hail Holy Queen

Hail, Holy Queen, Mother of mercy, our life, our sweetness, and our hope. To thee do we cry, poor banished children of Eve, to thee do we send up our sighs, mourning and weeping in this vale of tears. Turn then, most gracious advocate, thine eyes of mercy toward us; and after this our exile show unto us the blessed fruit of thy womb Jesus, O clement, O loving, O sweet Virgin Mary.

Pray for us, O holy Mother of God. That we may be made worthy of the promises of Christ.

O God, whose only begotten Son, by His life, death, and resurrection, has purchased for us the rewards of eternal salvation; grant we beseech Thee, that meditating upon these mysteries of the most holy Rosary of the Blessed Virgin Mary, we may imitate what they contain and obtain what they promise, through the same Christ our Lord.

Prayer to Our Lady of Guadalupe

Our Lady of Guadalupe, Mystical Rose, make intercession for the Holy Church, protect the Sovereign Pontiff, help all those who invoke thee in their necessities, and since thou art the Blessed Virgin Mary, and Mother of the True God, obtain for us from thy most holy Son the grace of keeping our faith, of sweet hope in the midst of the bitterness of life, of burning charity, and the most precious gift of perseverance so that we may carry our cross cheerfully.

St Josemaría Escrivá at the seminary of San Carlos in Zaragoza, 1922.

Day Eight: Detachment.

"Our Lord asks for generous hearts that are truly detached. We will achieve this if we resolutely cut the thick bonds or the subtle threads that tie us to ourselves. I won't hide from you the fact that this entails a constant struggle, overriding our own intelligence and will, a renunciation which, frankly, is more difficult than the giving up of the most prized material possessions. The detachment which Our Lord preached, and which He expects from every Christian, necessarily brings with it external manifestations. Jesus coepit facere et docere. Before teaching with words, He proclaimed His doctrine with deeds."

-St Josemaría Escrivá

Prayer Intention

Lord Jesus Christ, I desire to detach from what is not pleasing to You. If I should hunger, let me hunger for You. If I should sleep rough, let me sleep roughly for You. If I should feel heart break and scorn, let my heart break for You and let me be humiliated for You, Lord. I know that I cannot detach from what is distracting me from You, without your guidance and the love that flows from Your most Sacred Heart.

"Jesus Christ is the same yesterday and today and forever. Don't be led astray by various kinds of strange teachings; for it is good for the heart to be established by grace and not by foods, since those involved in them have not benefited."

- Hebrews 13:8-9

Day Eight: Detachment.

Dear Lord, I humbly beg You, through the intercession of St Josemaría Escrivá, for the grace to detach myself from that which distracts me from pleasing You. I ask that You detach me from all things offensive to You, and from all things that do not produce good fruit. Like the farmer who is dedicated to sowing his fields with fertile seeds and tending to his orchards, I must serve You from the sunrise until the sunset, sowing seeds of faith and charity.

Prayer to St Josemaría Escrivá

Most loving God, through the mediation of Our Lady, the Blessed Virgin, You chose St Josemaría Escrivá to serve You and honour you. You have gifted St Josemaría Escrivá the wisdom and grace to form Opus Dei, a way of sanctification in daily work and in the fulfilment of the Christian's ordinary life and duties. Grant that I too may learn to turn my everyday life into one that serves You God, and imitates the way of St Josemaría Escrivá with a zeal for loving all souls and striving for sanctification. Grant unto me God, through the intercession of St Josemaría Escrivá the favour of (intention).

Day Eight: Detachment.

"And with great power the apostles were giving their testimony to the resurrection of the Lord Jesus, and great grace was upon them all."

- Acts 4:33

Holy Rosary of Luminous Mysteries

I believe in God, the Father Almighty, Creator of Heaven, and earth; and in Jesus Christ, His only Son, Our Lord, who was conceived by the Holy Ghost, born of the Virgin Mary, suffered under Pontius Pilate, was crucified; died, and was buried. He descended into Hell; the third day He arose again from the dead; He ascended into Heaven, sitteth at the right hand of God, the Father Almighty; from thence He shall come to judge the living and the dead. I believe in the Holy Spirit, the holy Catholic Church, the communion of saints, the forgiveness of sins, the resurrection of the body, and life everlasting.

Our Father, who art in heaven, hallowed be Thy name; Thy kingdom come; Thy will be done on earth as it is in heaven. Give us this day our daily bread; and forgive us our trespasses as we forgive those who trespass against us; and lead us not into temptation, but deliver us from evil.

Hail Mary, full of grace. The Lord is with thee. Blessed art thou among women, and blessed is the fruit of thy womb, Jesus. Holy Mary, Mother of God, pray for us sinners, now and at the hour of our death.

Glory be to the Father, to the Son, and to the Holy Spirit, as it was, is now, and ever shall be, world without end. Amen.

The Five Luminous Mysteries are prayed on Thursday.

The Luminous Mysteries remind the faithful of Christ's shining light:

The Baptism in the River Jordan (Matthew 3:13–16); The Wedding Feast at Cana (John 2:1–11) The Preaching of the coming of the Kingdom of God (Mark 1:14–15) The Transfiguration (Matthew 17:1–8); The Institution of the Holy Eucharist (Matthew 26)

Hail Holy Queen

Hail, Holy Queen, Mother of mercy, our life, our sweetness, and our hope. To thee do we cry, poor banished children of Eve, to thee do we send up our sighs, mourning and weeping in this vale of tears. Turn then, most gracious advocate, thine eyes of mercy toward us; and after this our exile show unto us the blessed fruit of thy womb Jesus, O clement, O loving, O sweet Virgin Mary.

Pray for us, O holy Mother of God. That we may be made worthy of the promises of Christ.

O God, whose only begotten Son, by His life, death, and resurrection, has purchased for us the rewards of eternal salvation; grant we beseech Thee, that meditating upon these mysteries of the most holy Rosary of the Blessed Virgin Mary, we may imitate what they contain and obtain what they promise, through the same Christ our Lord.

Prayer to Our Lady of Guadalupe

Our Lady of Guadalupe, Mystical Rose, make intercession for the Holy Church, protect the Sovereign Pontiff, help all those who invoke thee in their necessities, and since thou art the Blessed Virgin Mary, and Mother of the True God, obtain for us from thy most holy Son the grace of keeping our faith, of sweet hope in the midst of the bitterness of life, of burning charity, and the most precious gift of perseverance so that we may carry our cross cheerfully.

St Josemaría Escrivá founded Opus Dei on October 2nd 1928 in Madrid.

Day Nine: Sincerity.

"When God runs toward us, we cannot keep silent, but with St Paul we exclaim: Abba, Pater: "Father, my Father!"...God is waiting for us, like the father in the parable, with open arms, even though we don't deserve it. It doesn't matter how great our debt is. Just like the prodigal son, all we must do is open our heart, to be homesick for our Father's house, to wonder at and rejoice in the gift which God makes us of being able to call ourselves his children, of really being His children, even though our response to Him has been so poor."

-St Josemaría Escrivá

Prayer Intention

Lord Jesus Christ, I desire to sincerely know You, to love You, and to serve You. I know that I cannot possibly accomplish that without true devotion to Your one Holy Apostolic Church. Please Lord, help me to stay sincere by keeping not just a strong faith but also proving my love to You through my works, my faith and through my obedience.

"But the Helper, the Holy Spirit, whom the Father will send in my name, He will teach you all things and bring to your remembrance all that I have said to you. Peace I leave with you, my peace I give unto you: not as the world giveth, give I unto you. Let not your heart be troubled, neither let it be afraid."

- John 14:26-27

Day Nine: Sincerity.

Dear Lord, I humbly beg You, through the intercession of St Josemaría Escrivá, for the grace to sincerely love You, to show this love not by my words alone but by my deeds as Your apostle St John instructed the little children to do. I too am the smallest of child in Your presence. Please Lord, help me to always live Your Truth with sincerity and zeal, compassionately sharing Your good news by being a sincere witness of Your love, mercy and sacrifice.

Prayer to St Josemaría Escrivá

Most loving God, through the mediation of Our Lady, the Blessed Virgin, You chose St Josemaría Escrivá to serve You and honour you. You have gifted St Josemaría Escrivá the wisdom and grace to form Opus Dei, a way of sanctification in daily work and in the fulfilment of the Christian's ordinary life and duties. Grant that I too may learn to turn my everyday life into one that serves You God, and imitates the way of St Josemaría Escrivá with a zeal for loving all souls and striving for sanctification. Grant unto me God, through the intercession of St Josemaría Escrivá the favour of (intention).

Day Nine: Sincerity.

"Summon your power, O God, the power, O God, by which you have worked for us."

- Psalm 68:28

Holy Rosary of Joyful Mysteries

I believe in God, the Father Almighty, Creator of Heaven, and earth; and in Jesus Christ, His only Son, Our Lord, who was conceived by the Holy Ghost, born of the Virgin Mary, suffered under Pontius Pilate, was crucified; died, and was buried. He descended into Hell; the third day He arose again from the dead; He ascended into Heaven, sitteth at the right hand of God, the Father Almighty; from thence He shall come to judge the living and the dead. I believe in the Holy Spirit, the holy Catholic Church, the communion of saints, the forgiveness of sins, the resurrection of the body, and life everlasting.

Our Father, who art in heaven, hallowed be Thy name; Thy kingdom come; Thy will be done on earth as it is in heaven. Give us this day our daily bread; and forgive us our trespasses as we forgive those who trespass against us; and lead us not into temptation, but deliver us from evil.

Hail Mary, full of grace. The Lord is with thee. Blessed art thou among women, and blessed is the fruit of thy womb, Jesus. Holy Mary, Mother of God, pray for us sinners, now and at the hour of our death.

Glory be to the Father, to the Son, and to the Holy Spirit, as it was, is now, and ever shall be, world without end. Amen.

The Five Joyful Mysteries are prayed Monday and Saturday.

The Joyful Mysteries remind the faithful of Our Lady's Fiat and Christ's birth:

The Annunciation (Luke 1:26–38); The Visitation (Luke 1:39–56) The Nativity (Luke 2:1–21); The Presentation (Luke 2:22–38) The Finding of the Child Jesus in the Temple (Luke 2:41–52)

Hail Holy Queen

Hail, Holy Queen, Mother of mercy, our life, our sweetness, and our hope. To thee do we cry, poor banished children of Eve, to thee do we send up our sighs, mourning and weeping in this vale of tears. Turn then, most gracious advocate, thine eyes of mercy toward us; and after this our exile show unto us the blessed fruit of thy womb Jesus, O clement, O loving, O sweet Virgin Mary.

Pray for us, O holy Mother of God. That we may be made worthy of the promises of Christ.

O God, whose only begotten Son, by His life, death, and resurrection, has purchased for us the rewards of eternal salvation; grant we beseech Thee, that meditating upon these mysteries of the most holy Rosary of the Blessed Virgin Mary, we may imitate what they contain and obtain what they promise, through the same Christ our Lord.

Prayer to Our Lady of Guadalupe

Our Lady of Guadalupe, Mystical Rose, make intercession for the Holy Church, protect the Sovereign Pontiff, help all those who invoke thee in their necessities, and since thou art the Blessed Virgin Mary, and Mother of the True God, obtain for us from thy most holy Son the grace of keeping our faith, of sweet hope in the midst of the bitterness of life, of burning charity, and the most precious gift of perseverance so that we may carry our cross cheerfully.

St Josemaría Escrivá with Blessed Alvaro del Portillo in 1939.

Day Ten: Generosity.

"What holy resources poverty has! Do you remember? It was a time of financial distress for that apostolic undertaking, and you had given without stint down to your last penny. And he, a priest of God, said to you: 'I too will give you all that I have,' You knelt, and heard: 'May the blessing of almighty God, the Father, the Son and the Holy Spirit, descend upon you and remain with you for ever'. You are still convinced that you were well paid."

-St Josemaría Escrivá

Prayer Intention

Lord Jesus Christ, I desire to always show my gratitude by giving to Your most holy church. If it is Your will dear Lord, that I should be left so poor and destitute like the man named Lazarus, that even then, I will never keep for myself more than what I give unto You. To love thy neighbour by way of alms giving is to love You, Lord Jesus Christ. I know through Your mercy and love that I can bear witness.

"Now this I say, he who sows sparingly will also reap sparingly, and he who sows bountifully will also reap bountifully. Each one must do just as he has purposed in his heart, not grudgingly or under compulsion, for God loves a cheerful giver. And God is able to make every grace overflow to you, so that in every way, always having everything you need, you may excel in every good work."

- 2 Corinthians 9:6-8

Day Ten: Generosity.

Dear Lord, I humbly beg You, through the intercession of St Josemaría Escrivá, for the grace to always see You within those most in need; the poor, the ill, the hungry, and the Church in need of volunteers so that it can function to better carry out its mission and be a sanctuary to those souls most in need of Your shelter and of Your infinite compassion.

Prayer to St Josemaría Escrivá

Most loving God, through the mediation of Our Lady, the Blessed Virgin, You chose St Josemaría Escrivá to serve You and honour you. You have gifted St Josemaría Escrivá the wisdom and grace to form Opus Dei, a way of sanctification in daily work and in the fulfilment of the Christian's ordinary life and duties. Grant that I too may learn to turn my everyday life into one that serves You God, and imitates the way of St Josemaría Escrivá with a zeal for loving all souls and striving for sanctification. Grant unto me God, through the intercession of St Josemaría Escrivá the favour of (intention).

Day Ten: Generosity.

Jesus said to him, "If you would be perfect, go, sell what you possess and give to the poor, and you will have treasure in Heaven; and come, follow me."

- Matthew 19:21

Holy Rosary of Sorrowful Mysteries

I believe in God, the Father Almighty, Creator of Heaven, and earth; and in Jesus Christ, His only Son, Our Lord, who was conceived by the Holy Ghost, born of the Virgin Mary, suffered under Pontius Pilate, was crucified; died, and was buried. He descended into Hell; the third day He arose again from the dead; He ascended into Heaven, sitteth at the right hand of God, the Father Almighty; from thence He shall come to judge the living and the dead. I believe in the Holy Spirit, the holy Catholic Church, the communion of saints, the forgiveness of sins, the resurrection of the body, and life everlasting.

Our Father, who art in heaven, hallowed be Thy name; Thy kingdom come; Thy will be done on earth as it is in heaven. Give us this day our daily bread; and forgive us our trespasses as we forgive those who trespass against us; and lead us not into temptation, but deliver us from evil.

Hail Mary, full of grace. The Lord is with thee. Blessed art thou among women, and blessed is the fruit of thy womb, Jesus. Holy Mary, Mother of God, pray for us sinners, now and at the hour of our death.

Glory be to the Father, to the Son, and to the Holy Spirit, as it was, is now, and ever shall be, world without end. Amen.

The Five Sorrowful Mysteries are prayed Tuesday and Friday.

The Sorrowful Mysteries remind the faithful of Christ's Passion and of His Crucifixion:

The Agony of Jesus in the Garden (Matthew 26:36–56); The Scourging at the Pillar (Matthew 27:26) The Crowning with Thorns (Matthew 27:27–31); The Carrying of the Cross (Matthew 27:32) The Crucifixion (Matthew 27:33–56)

Hail Holy Queen

Hail, Holy Queen, Mother of mercy, our life, our sweetness, and our hope. To thee do we cry, poor banished children of Eve, to thee do we send up our sighs, mourning and weeping in this vale of tears. Turn then, most gracious advocate, thine eyes of mercy toward us; and after this our exile show unto us the blessed fruit of thy womb Jesus, O clement, O loving, O sweet Virgin Mary.

Pray for us, O holy Mother of God. That we may be made worthy of the promises of Christ.

O God, whose only begotten Son, by His life, death, and resurrection, has purchased for us the rewards of eternal salvation; grant we beseech Thee, that meditating upon these mysteries of the most holy Rosary of the Blessed Virgin Mary, we may imitate what they contain and obtain what they promise, through the same Christ our Lord.

Prayer to Our Lady of Guadalupe

Our Lady of Guadalupe, Mystical Rose, make intercession for the Holy Church, protect the Sovereign Pontiff, help all those who invoke thee in their necessities, and since thou art the Blessed Virgin Mary, and Mother of the True God, obtain for us from thy most holy Son the grace of keeping our faith, of sweet hope in the midst of the bitterness of life, of burning charity, and the most precious gift of perseverance so that we may carry our cross cheerfully.

St Josemaría Escrivá and Blessed Alvaro del Portillo, late 1930's during the Spanish Civil War.

Day Eleven: Chastity and Modesty.

"The bonus odor Christi, the fragrance of Christ, is also that of our clean life, of our chastity — the chastity of each one in his own state, I repeat — of our holy purity, which is a joyful affirmation. It is something solid and at the same time gentle; it is refined, avoiding even the use of inappropriate words, since they cannot be pleasing to God."

-St Josemaría Escrivá

Prayer Intention

Lord Jesus Christ, I desire to be modest and chaste in my thoughts, deed, and words. I was baptised as a Christian which washed away the original sin from my soul and renewed me as Your child. I know that without the sacraments, I cannot possibly remain steadfast in chastity. Oh, how the slightest temptation toward sin can separate us from You. Please Lord Jesus, I ask that You give me the strength and fortitude to stay focused on that which pleases You, Lord.

"Do not be conformed to this world, but be transformed by the renewal of your mind, that by testing you may discern what is the will of God, what is good and acceptable and perfect. For by the grace given to me, I tell everyone among you not to think of himself more highly than he should think. Instead, think sensibly, as God has distributed a measure of faith to each one."

- Romans 12:2-3

Day Eleven: Chastity and Modesty.

Dear Lord, I humbly beg You, through the intercession of St Josemaría Escrivá, for the grace to remember You when satan beckons me to sin against modesty and chastity. You taught the world how to truly love through devotion to You, and what true love is, compared to what is spiritual harm merely disguised as love.

Prayer to St Josemaría Escrivá

Most loving God, through the mediation of Our Lady, the Blessed Virgin, You chose St Josemaría Escrivá to serve You and honour you. You have gifted St Josemaría Escrivá the wisdom and grace to form Opus Dei, a way of sanctification in daily work and in the fulfilment of the Christian's ordinary life and duties. Grant that I too may learn to turn my everyday life into one that serves You God, and imitates the way of St Josemaría Escrivá with a zeal for loving all souls and striving for sanctification. Grant unto me God, through the intercession of St Josemaría Escrivá the favour of (intention).

Day Eleven: Chastity & Modesty.

"Put to death therefore what is earthly in you: sexual immorality, impurity, passion, evil desire, and covetousness, which is idolatry."

- Colossians 3:5

Holy Rosary of Glorious Mysteries

I believe in God, the Father Almighty, Creator of Heaven, and earth; and in Jesus Christ, His only Son, Our Lord, who was conceived by the Holy Ghost, born of the Virgin Mary, suffered under Pontius Pilate, was crucified; died, and was buried. He descended into Hell; the third day He arose again from the dead; He ascended into Heaven, sitteth at the right hand of God, the Father Almighty; from thence He shall come to judge the living and the dead. I believe in the Holy Spirit, the holy Catholic Church, the communion of saints, the forgiveness of sins, the resurrection of the body, and life everlasting.

Our Father, who art in heaven, hallowed be Thy name; Thy kingdom come; Thy will be done on earth as it is in heaven. Give us this day our daily bread; and forgive us our trespasses as we forgive those who trespass against us; and lead us not into temptation, but deliver us from evil.

Hail Mary, full of grace. The Lord is with thee. Blessed art thou among women, and blessed is the fruit of thy womb, Jesus. Holy Mary, Mother of God, pray for us sinners, now and at the hour of our death.

Glory be to the Father, to the Son, and to the Holy Spirit, as it was, is now, and ever shall be, world without end. Amen.

The Five Glorious Mysteries are prayed Wednesday and Sunday.

The Glorious Mysteries remind the faithful of Christ's Resurrection and Heaven's glories:

The Resurrection (Luke 24:1-12); The Ascension (Acts 1:6-11) The Descent of the Holy Spirit (Acts 2:1-4); The Assumption (Munificentissimus Deus 44) The Coronation of Mary as Queen of Heaven (Revelations 12:1-6)

Hail Holy Queen

Hail, Holy Queen, Mother of mercy, our life, our sweetness, and our hope. To thee do we cry, poor banished children of Eve, to thee do we send up our sighs, mourning and weeping in this vale of tears. Turn then, most gracious advocate, thine eyes of mercy toward us; and after this our exile show unto us the blessed fruit of thy womb Jesus, O clement, O loving, O sweet Virgin Mary.

Pray for us, O holy Mother of God. That we may be made worthy of the promises of Christ.

O God, whose only begotten Son, by His life, death, and resurrection, has purchased for us the rewards of eternal salvation; grant we beseech Thee, that meditating upon these mysteries of the most holy Rosary of the Blessed Virgin Mary, we may imitate what they contain and obtain what they promise, through the same Christ our Lord.

Prayer to Our Lady of Guadalupe

Our Lady of Guadalupe, Mystical Rose, make intercession for the Holy Church, protect the Sovereign Pontiff, help all those who invoke thee in their necessities, and since thou art the Blessed Virgin Mary, and Mother of the True God, obtain for us from thy most holy Son the grace of keeping our faith, of sweet hope in the midst of the bitterness of life, of burning charity, and the most precious gift of perseverance so that we may carry our cross cheerfully.

St Josemaría Escrivá & Bishop of Madrid, Leopoldo Eijo y Garay in 1943.

Day Twelve: Obedience.

"With God, who does not lose battles, we will always be the victors. That is why in the struggle for sanctity, if you feel lacking in strength, you should listen to the commands, do what you are told, let yourself be helped... for He does not fail."

-St Josemaría Escrivá

Prayer Intention

Lord Jesus Christ, I desire to humble myself and be more obedient to Your will. I cannot do this without humility and a heart that strives for the salvation of souls, and for the good of the Church. I ask that You continue to lead me to obedience, especially toward those You have chosen to be in a position of spiritual authority, acting on Your behalf. Obedience to Your most holy will means to submit to the teachings of the Church and to the shepherds which through their apostolic succession, help lead the flock to sainthood.

"Obey your leaders and submit to them, for they are keeping watch over your souls, as those who will have to give an account. Let them do this with joy and not with groaning, for that would be of no advantage to you. Pray for us: for we trust we have a good conscience, in all things willing to live honestly. And I urge all of you to pray earnestly, so that I may be restored to you soon. Now the God of peace, that brought again from the dead our Lord Jesus, that great shepherd of the sheep, through the blood of the everlasting covenant."

- Hebrews 13:17-20

Day Twelve: Obedience.

Dear Lord, I humbly beg You, through the intercession of St Josemaría Escrivá, for the grace of obedience. I know that I can through spiritual reading, attending the sacraments and Mass regularly, along with prayer, attain this. Thank You Lord, for the wisdom of the Saints, especially those who spoke and wrote most of the freedom of being obedient to the Church and to Your will, all of whom are shining examples of obedience to Your divine Church.

Prayer to St Josemaría Escrivá

Most loving God, through the mediation of Our Lady, the Blessed Virgin, You chose St Josemaría Escrivá to serve You and honour you. You have gifted St Josemaría Escrivá the wisdom and grace to form Opus Dei, a way of sanctification in daily work and in the fulfilment of the Christian's ordinary life and duties. Grant that I too may learn to turn my everyday life into one that serves You God, and imitates the way of St Josemaría Escrivá with a zeal for loving all souls and striving for sanctification. Grant unto me God, through the intercession of St Josemaría Escrivá the favour of (intention).

Day Twelve: Obedience.

"Put to death therefore what is earthly in you: sexual immorality, impurity, passion, evil desire, and covetousness, which is idolatry."

- Colossians 3:5

Holy Rosary of Luminous Mysteries

I believe in God, the Father Almighty, Creator of Heaven, and earth; and in Jesus Christ, His only Son, Our Lord, who was conceived by the Holy Ghost, born of the Virgin Mary, suffered under Pontius Pilate, was crucified; died, and was buried. He descended into Hell; the third day He arose again from the dead; He ascended into Heaven, sitteth at the right hand of God, the Father Almighty; from thence He shall come to judge the living and the dead. I believe in the Holy Spirit, the holy Catholic Church, the communion of saints, the forgiveness of sins, the resurrection of the body, and life everlasting.

Our Father, who art in heaven, hallowed be Thy name; Thy kingdom come; Thy will be done on earth as it is in heaven. Give us this day our daily bread; and forgive us our trespasses as we forgive those who trespass against us; and lead us not into temptation, but deliver us from evil.

Hail Mary, full of grace. The Lord is with thee. Blessed art thou among women, and blessed is the fruit of thy womb, Jesus. Holy Mary, Mother of God, pray for us sinners, now and at the hour of our death.

Glory be to the Father, to the Son, and to the Holy Spirit, as it was, is now, and ever shall be, world without end. Amen.

The Five Luminous Mysteries are prayed on Thursday.

The Luminous Mysteries remind the faithful of Christ's shining light:

The Baptism in the River Jordan (Matthew 3:13–16); The Wedding Feast at Cana (John 2:1–11) The Preaching of the coming of the Kingdom of God (Mark 1:14–15) The Transfiguration (Matthew 17:1–8); The Institution of the Holy Eucharist (Matthew 26)

Hail Holy Queen

Hail, Holy Queen, Mother of mercy, our life, our sweetness, and our hope. To thee do we cry, poor banished children of Eve, to thee do we send up our sighs, mourning and weeping in this vale of tears. Turn then, most gracious advocate, thine eyes of mercy toward us; and after this our exile show unto us the blessed fruit of thy womb Jesus, O clement, O loving, O sweet Virgin Mary.

Pray for us, O holy Mother of God. That we may be made worthy of the promises of Christ.

O God, whose only begotten Son, by His life, death, and resurrection, has purchased for us the rewards of eternal salvation; grant we beseech Thee, that meditating upon these mysteries of the most holy Rosary of the Blessed Virgin Mary, we may imitate what they contain and obtain what they promise, through the same Christ our Lord.

Prayer to Our Lady of Guadalupe

Our Lady of Guadalupe, Mystical Rose, make intercession for the Holy Church, protect the Sovereign Pontiff, help all those who invoke thee in their necessities, and since thou art the Blessed Virgin Mary, and Mother of the True God, obtain for us from thy most holy Son the grace of keeping our faith, of sweet hope in the midst of the bitterness of life, of burning charity, and the most precious gift of perseverance so that we may carry our cross cheerfully.

St Josemaría Escrivá with the mother of saints
Francisco & Jacinta Marto at Fatima in 1945.

Day Thirteen: Mortification.

"When you see a poor wooden Cross, alone, uncared for, and of no value... and without its Crucified, don't forget that that Cross is your Cross: The Cross of each day, the hidden Cross, without splendour or consolation...The Cross which is awaiting the Crucified it lacks: and that Crucified must be you."

-St Josemaría Escrivá

Prayer Intention

Lord Jesus Christ, I desire to carry my cross with gratitude and bear the weight, which may be at times heavy, but will not crush my bones. I cannot bear the weight of my cross and endure even simple acts of mortification without Your grace dear Lord. At times when I feel burdened and think of giving up, I will remember that You never gave up because You love me and were crucified for my redemption.

"Jesus said to him; "I am the way, and the truth, and the life. No one comes to the Father except through me. If you had known Me, you would have known My Father also; from now on you know Him and have seen Him. "Lord," said Philip, "show us the Father, and that's enough for us. Jesus said to him, "Have I been so long with you, and yet you have not come to know Me, Philip? He who has seen Me has seen the Father; how can you say, 'Show us the Father'?"

- John 14:6-9

Day Thirteen: Mortification.

Dear Lord, I humbly beg You, through the intercession of St Josemaría Escrivá, for the grace to endure mortification. Thank You Lord, for Your loving mercy and compassion. Through all acts of mortification, I allow my heart to and my soul to fall in love with The Cross on which You were crucified for the salvation of all souls.

Prayer to St Josemaría Escrivá

Most loving God, through the mediation of Our Lady, the Blessed Virgin, You chose St Josemaría Escrivá to serve You and honour you. You have gifted St Josemaría Escrivá the wisdom and grace to form Opus Dei, a way of sanctification in daily work and in the fulfilment of the Christian's ordinary life and duties. Grant that I too may learn to turn my everyday life into one that serves You God, and imitates the way of St Josemaría Escrivá with a zeal for loving all souls and striving for sanctification. Grant unto me God, through the intercession of St Josemaría Escrivá the favour of (intention).

Day Thirteen: Mortification.

"Let the word of Christ dwell in you richly, teaching and admonishing one another in all wisdom, singing psalms and hymns and spiritual songs, with thankfulness in your hearts to God."

- Colossians 3:16

Holy Rosary of Joyful Mysteries

I believe in God, the Father Almighty, Creator of Heaven, and earth; and in Jesus Christ, His only Son, Our Lord, who was conceived by the Holy Ghost, born of the Virgin Mary, suffered under Pontius Pilate, was crucified; died, and was buried. He descended into Hell; the third day He arose again from the dead; He ascended into Heaven, sitteth at the right hand of God, the Father Almighty; from thence He shall come to judge the living and the dead. I believe in the Holy Spirit, the holy Catholic Church, the communion of saints, the forgiveness of sins, the resurrection of the body, and life everlasting.

Our Father, who art in heaven, hallowed be Thy name; Thy kingdom come; Thy will be done on earth as it is in heaven. Give us this day our daily bread; and forgive us our trespasses as we forgive those who trespass against us; and lead us not into temptation, but deliver us from evil.

Hail Mary, full of grace. The Lord is with thee. Blessed art thou among women, and blessed is the fruit of thy womb, Jesus. Holy Mary, Mother of God, pray for us sinners, now and at the hour of our death.

Glory be to the Father, to the Son, and to the Holy Spirit, as it was, is now, and ever shall be, world without end. Amen.

The Five Joyful Mysteries are prayed Monday and Saturday.

The Joyful Mysteries remind the faithful of Our Lady's Fiat and Christ's birth:

The Annunciation (Luke 1:26–38); The Visitation (Luke 1:39–56) The Nativity (Luke 2:1–21); The Presentation (Luke 2:22–38) The Finding of the Child Jesus in the Temple (Luke 2:41–52)

Hail Holy Queen

Hail, Holy Queen, Mother of mercy, our life, our sweetness, and our hope. To thee do we cry, poor banished children of Eve, to thee do we send up our sighs, mourning and weeping in this vale of tears. Turn then, most gracious advocate, thine eyes of mercy toward us; and after this our exile show unto us the blessed fruit of thy womb Jesus, O clement, O loving, O sweet Virgin Mary.

Pray for us, O holy Mother of God. That we may be made worthy of the promises of Christ.

O God, whose only begotten Son, by His life, death, and resurrection, has purchased for us the rewards of eternal salvation; grant we beseech Thee, that meditating upon these mysteries of the most holy Rosary of the Blessed Virgin Mary, we may imitate what they contain and obtain what they promise, through the same Christ our Lord.

Prayer to Our Lady of Guadalupe

Our Lady of Guadalupe, Mystical Rose, make intercession for the Holy Church, protect the Sovereign Pontiff, help all those who invoke thee in their necessities, and since thou art the Blessed Virgin Mary, and Mother of the True God, obtain for us from thy most holy Son the grace of keeping our faith, of sweet hope in the midst of the bitterness of life, of burning charity, and the most precious gift of perseverance so that we may carry our cross cheerfully.

St Josemaría Escrivá with members of Opus Dei in 1949.

Day Fourteen: Plan of Life.

"This tying of one's life to a plan, to a timetable, you tell me, is so monotonous! And I answer: there is monotony because there is little Love."

-St Josemaría Escrivá

Prayer Intention

Lord Jesus Christ, I desire to manage my life according to Your will. Each day is to be carefully planned in a way which is focused on You dear Lord. When I awake every morning to the warm sunrise, what a blessing it is. To go study or work, knowing that too, is for you, dear Jesus. Nothing when done for You Lord, is ever boring or monotonous. Our ordinary life is a precious gift, so, we must live it well.

"And we know that for those who love God, all things work together for good, for those who are called according to His purpose. For those whom He foreknew, He also predestined to become conformed to the image of His Son, so that He would be the firstborn among many brethren. And these whom He predestined, He also called; and these whom He called, He also justified; and these whom He justified, He also glorified. What then shall we say to these things? If God is for us, who is against us? He who did not spare His own Son, but delivered Him over for us all, how will He not also with Him freely give us all things?"

- Romans 8:28-30

Day Fourteen: Plan of Life.

Dear Lord, I humbly beg You, through the intercession of St Josemaría Escrivá, for the grace to lead me each day through my plan of life. From the moment I wake in the morning, through all tasks and up to the moment that I lay down to sleep. Keep my heart dear Lord, filled with gratitude and happiness so that I can do my daily routine prayerfully, sanctifying my ordinary life with good cheer.

Prayer to St Josemaría Escrivá

Most loving God, through the mediation of Our Lady, the Blessed Virgin, You chose St Josemaría Escrivá to serve You and honour you. You have gifted St Josemaría Escrivá the wisdom and grace to form Opus Dei, a way of sanctification in daily work and in the fulfilment of the Christian's ordinary life and duties. Grant that I too may learn to turn my everyday life into one that serves You God, and imitates the way of St Josemaría Escrivá with a zeal for loving all souls and striving for sanctification. Grant unto me God, through the intercession of St Josemaría Escrivá the favour of (intention).

Day Fourteen: Plan of Life.

"Do your best to present yourself to God as one approved, a worker who has no need to be ashamed, rightly handling the word of truth."

- 2 Timothy 2:15

Holy Rosary of Sorrowful Mysteries

I believe in God, the Father Almighty, Creator of Heaven and earth; and in Jesus Christ, His only Son, Our Lord, who was conceived by the Holy Ghost, born of the Virgin Mary, suffered under Pontius Pilate, was crucified; died, and was buried. He descended into Hell; the third day He arose again from the dead; He ascended into Heaven, sitteth at the right hand of God, the Father Almighty; from thence He shall come to judge the living and the dead. I believe in the Holy Spirit, the holy Catholic Church, the communion of saints, the forgiveness of sins, the resurrection of the body, and life everlasting.

Our Father, who art in heaven, hallowed be Thy name; Thy kingdom come; Thy will be done on earth as it is in heaven. Give us this day our daily bread; and forgive us our trespasses as we forgive those who trespass against us; and lead us not into temptation, but deliver us from evil.

Hail Mary, full of grace. The Lord is with thee. Blessed art thou among women, and blessed is the fruit of thy womb, Jesus. Holy Mary, Mother of God, pray for us sinners, now and at the hour of our death.

Glory be to the Father, to the Son, and to the Holy Spirit, as it was, is now, and ever shall be, world without end. Amen.

The Five Sorrowful Mysteries are prayed Tuesday and Friday.

The Sorrowful Mysteries remind the faithful of Christ's Passion and of His Crucifixion:

The Agony of Jesus in the Garden (Matthew 26:36–56); The Scourging at the Pillar (Matthew 27:26) The Crowning with Thorns (Matthew 27:27–31); The Carrying of the Cross (Matthew 27:32) The Crucifixion (Matthew 27:33–56)

Hail Holy Queen

Hail, Holy Queen, Mother of mercy, our life, our sweetness, and our hope. To thee do we cry, poor banished children of Eve, to thee do we send up our sighs, mourning and weeping in this vale of tears. Turn then, most gracious advocate, thine eyes of mercy toward us; and after this our exile show unto us the blessed fruit of thy womb Jesus, O clement, O loving, O sweet Virgin Mary.

Pray for us, O holy Mother of God. That we may be made worthy of the promises of Christ.

O God, whose only begotten Son, by His life, death, and resurrection, has purchased for us the rewards of eternal salvation; grant we beseech Thee, that meditating upon these mysteries of the most holy Rosary of the Blessed Virgin Mary, we may imitate what they contain and obtain what they promise, through the same Christ our Lord.

Prayer to Our Lady of Guadalupe

Our Lady of Guadalupe, Mystical Rose, make intercession for the Holy Church, protect the Sovereign Pontiff, help all those who invoke thee in their necessities, and since thou art the Blessed Virgin Mary, and Mother of the True God, obtain for us from thy most holy Son the grace of keeping our faith, of sweet hope in the midst of the bitterness of life, of burning charity, and the most precious gift of perseverance so that we may carry our cross cheerfully.

St Josemaría Escrivá arrives in Vienna for the very first time, in 1955.

Day Fifteen: Poverty.

"Naturally, you have to use earthly means, but put a lot of effort into being detached from everything of the earth, so that you can deal with it with your mind always fixed on the service of God and of your fellow men."

-St Josemaría Escrivá

Prayer Intention

Lord Jesus Christ, I desire to serve You and give to You all that I hold dear. I don't need anything beyond basic needs to sustain life and to carry out my duties in serving You. Everything else is a gift from You which I do not deserve. When the poor and hungry want for food, if it is Your will and I have the means, I shall feed them as You feed me with the Bread of Life, dear Lord Jesus. May the poor also find shelter and be fed with Your word and Your wisdom through Christian charity, bearing witness in loving our neighbour.

"It is not for kings, O Lemuel, it is not for kings to drink wine; nor for princes strong drink: Lest they drink, and forget the law, and pervert the judgment of any of the afflicted. Give strong drink unto him that is ready to perish, and wine unto those that be of heavy hearts. Let him drink, and forget his poverty, and remember his misery no more. Open your mouth for the mute, for the rights of all who are destitute. Open your mouth, judge righteously, defend the rights of the poor and needy."

- Proverbs 31:4-9

Day Fifteen: Poverty.

Dear Lord, I humbly beg You, through the intercession of St Josemaría Escrivá, to allow me to live as though I have very little, even if I am well above my means. At times when I may want for something very expensive, remind me of the hungry and the poor, and what I can do for them instead, out of Christian charity and love, which pleases You, rather than indulge myself in greed and gluttony out of selfishness.

Prayer to St Josemaría Escrivá

Most loving God, through the mediation of Our Lady, the Blessed Virgin, You chose St Josemaría Escrivá to serve You and honour you. You have gifted St Josemaría Escrivá the wisdom and grace to form Opus Dei, a way of sanctification in daily work and in the fulfilment of the Christian's ordinary life and duties. Grant that I too may learn to turn my everyday life into one that serves You God, and imitates the way of St Josemaría Escrivá with a zeal for loving all souls and striving for sanctification. Grant unto me God, through the intercession of St Josemaría Escrivá the favour of (intention).

Day Fifteen: Poverty.

"And he lifted up his eyes on his disciples, and said: "Blessed are you who are poor, for yours is the kingdom of God. Blessed are you who are hungry now, for you shall be satisfied." "Blessed are you who weep now, for you shall laugh."

- Luke 6:20-21

Holy Rosary of Glorious Mysteries

I believe in God, the Father Almighty, Creator of Heaven, and earth; and in Jesus Christ, His only Son, Our Lord, who was conceived by the Holy Ghost, born of the Virgin Mary, suffered under Pontius Pilate, was crucified; died, and was buried. He descended into Hell; the third day He arose again from the dead; He ascended into Heaven, sitteth at the right hand of God, the Father Almighty; from thence He shall come to judge the living and the dead. I believe in the Holy Spirit, the holy Catholic Church, the communion of saints, the forgiveness of sins, the resurrection of the body, and life everlasting.

Our Father, who art in heaven, hallowed be Thy name; Thy kingdom come; Thy will be done on earth as it is in heaven. Give us this day our daily bread; and forgive us our trespasses as we forgive those who trespass against us; and lead us not into temptation, but deliver us from evil.

Hail Mary, full of grace. The Lord is with thee. Blessed art thou among women, and blessed is the fruit of thy womb, Jesus. Holy Mary, Mother of God, pray for us sinners, now and at the hour of our death.

Glory be to the Father, to the Son, and to the Holy Spirit, as it was, is now, and ever shall be, world without end. Amen.

The Five Glorious Mysteries are prayed Wednesday and Sunday.

The Glorious Mysteries remind the faithful of Christ's Resurrection and Heaven's glories:

The Resurrection (Luke 24:1-12); The Ascension (Acts 1:6-11) The Descent of the Holy Spirit (Acts 2:1-4); The Assumption (Munificentissimus Deus 44) The Coronation of Mary as Queen of Heaven (Revelations 12:1-6)

Hail Holy Queen

Hail, Holy Queen, Mother of mercy, our life, our sweetness, and our hope. To thee do we cry, poor banished children of Eve, to thee do we send up our sighs, mourning and weeping in this vale of tears. Turn then, most gracious advocate, thine eyes of mercy toward us; and after this our exile show unto us the blessed fruit of thy womb Jesus, O clement, O loving, O sweet Virgin Mary.

Pray for us, O holy Mother of God. That we may be made worthy of the promises of Christ.

O God, whose only begotten Son, by His life, death, and resurrection, has purchased for us the rewards of eternal salvation; grant we beseech Thee, that meditating upon these mysteries of the most holy Rosary of the Blessed Virgin Mary, we may imitate what they contain and obtain what they promise, through the same Christ our Lord.

Prayer to Our Lady of Guadalupe

Our Lady of Guadalupe, Mystical Rose, make intercession for the Holy Church, protect the Sovereign Pontiff, help all those who invoke thee in their necessities, and since thou art the Blessed Virgin Mary, and Mother of the True God, obtain for us from thy most holy Son the grace of keeping our faith, of sweet hope in the midst of the bitterness of life, of burning charity, and the most precious gift of perseverance so that we may carry our cross cheerfully.

St Josemaría Escrivá with members of Opus Dei.

Day Sixteen: Fidelity.

"There are many people around you, and you have no right to be an obstacle to their spiritual good, to their eternal happiness. You are under an obligation to be a Saint. You must not let God down for having chosen you. Neither must you let those around you down: they expect so much from your Christian life."

-St Josemaría Escrivá

Prayer Intention

Lord Jesus Christ, I desire to be faithful to You and the Church always, even through my darkest nights. I know that I cannot do this without regularly attending the sacraments and Mass. I must have faith in all that You will. Through my blessings and suffering I will be strengthened, and my faith shall grow. I know that I can always turn to You dear Lord, who will never stop loving me and wanting for me to serve You and my brothers and sisters of the Church faithfully out of love and free will.

"Not pilfering, but showing all good faith, so that in everything, they may adorn the doctrine of God our Saviour. For the grace of God has appeared, bringing salvation to all people. It trains us to renounce ungodly living and worldly passions so that we might live sensible, honest, and godly lives in the present age as we wait for the blessed hope and glorious appearance of our great God and Saviour, Jesus the Messiah."

- Titus 2:10-13

Day Sixteen: Fidelity.

Dear Lord, I humbly beg You, through the intercession of St Josemaría Escrivá, Your humble and faithful servant, for the grace to live my life each day faithfully. That I may never fall into the snares of the devil and be lead astray from You dear Lord, for all I need to know and trust is in You and in Your Holy Church.

Prayer to St Josemaría Escrivá

Most loving God, through the mediation of Our Lady, the Blessed Virgin, You chose St Josemaría Escrivá to serve You and honour you. You have gifted St Josemaría Escrivá the wisdom and grace to form Opus Dei, a way of sanctification in daily work and in the fulfilment of the Christian's ordinary life and duties. Grant that I too may learn to turn my everyday life into one that serves You God, and imitates the way of St Josemaría Escrivá with a zeal for loving all souls and striving for sanctification. Grant unto me God, through the intercession of St Josemaría Escrivá the favour of (intention).

Day Sixteen: Fidelity.

"Know therefore that the Lord your God is God, the faithful God who keeps covenant and steadfast love with those who love Him and keep His commandments, to a thousand generations."

- Deuteronomy 7:9

Holy Rosary of Luminous Mysteries

I believe in God, the Father Almighty, Creator of Heaven, and earth; and in Jesus Christ, His only Son, Our Lord, who was conceived by the Holy Ghost, born of the Virgin Mary, suffered under Pontius Pilate, was crucified; died, and was buried. He descended into Hell; the third day He arose again from the dead; He ascended into Heaven, sitteth at the right hand of God, the Father Almighty; from thence He shall come to judge the living and the dead. I believe in the Holy Spirit, the holy Catholic Church, the communion of saints, the forgiveness of sins, the resurrection of the body, and life everlasting.

Our Father, who art in heaven, hallowed be Thy name; Thy kingdom come; Thy will be done on earth as it is in heaven. Give us this day our daily bread; and forgive us our trespasses as we forgive those who trespass against us; and lead us not into temptation, but deliver us from evil.

Hail Mary, full of grace. The Lord is with thee. Blessed art thou among women, and blessed is the fruit of thy womb, Jesus. Holy Mary, Mother of God, pray for us sinners, now and at the hour of our death.

Glory be to the Father, to the Son, and to the Holy Spirit, as it was, is now, and ever shall be, world without end. Amen.

The Five Luminous Mysteries are prayed on Thursday.

The Luminous Mysteries remind the faithful of Christ's shining light:

The Baptism in the River Jordan (Matthew 3:13–16); The Wedding Feast at Cana (John 2:1–11) The Preaching of the coming of the Kingdom of God (Mark 1:14–15) The Transfiguration (Matthew 17:1–8); The Institution of the Holy Eucharist (Matthew 26)

Hail Holy Queen

Hail, Holy Queen, Mother of mercy, our life, our sweetness, and our hope. To thee do we cry, poor banished children of Eve, to thee do we send up our sighs, mourning and weeping in this vale of tears. Turn then, most gracious advocate, thine eyes of mercy toward us; and after this our exile show unto us the blessed fruit of thy womb Jesus, O clement, O loving, O sweet Virgin Mary.

Pray for us, O holy Mother of God. That we may be made worthy of the promises of Christ.

O God, whose only begotten Son, by His life, death, and resurrection, has purchased for us the rewards of eternal salvation; grant we beseech Thee, that meditating upon these mysteries of the most holy Rosary of the Blessed Virgin Mary, we may imitate what they contain and obtain what they promise, through the same Christ our Lord.

Prayer to Our Lady of Guadalupe

Our Lady of Guadalupe, Mystical Rose, make intercession for the Holy Church, protect the Sovereign Pontiff, help all those who invoke thee in their necessities, and since thou art the Blessed Virgin Mary, and Mother of the True God, obtain for us from thy most holy Son the grace of keeping our faith, of sweet hope in the midst of the bitterness of life, of burning charity, and the most precious gift of perseverance so that we may carry our cross cheerfully.

St Josemaría Escrivá with Blessed Alvaro del Portillo and Javier Echevarría Rodríguez in Canterbury England, visiting St Dunstan's church, the shrine of St Thomas More in 1958.

Day Seventeen: Rest & Recovery.

"Remember that God loves His creatures to distraction. How can a donkey work if it is not fed or given enough rest, or if its spirit is broken by too many beatings? Well, your body is like a little donkey, and it was a donkey that was God's chosen throne in Jerusalem, and it carries you along the divine pathways of this earth of ours. But it has to be controlled so that it doesn't stray away from God's paths."

-St Josemaría Escrivá

Prayer Intention

Lord Jesus Christ, I desire to serve You even when I am exhausted. I know that I can still find ways during my days of rest, to carry out my duties as a Christian in service to Your Church. I can do this by attending retreats, engaging in peaceful spiritual readings and recollections, in adoration of the Blessed Sacrament, praying the Holy Rosary and giving thanks for all that You give to me, for You alone are peace, dear Lord.

"Stand in awe, and sin not: commune with your own heart upon your bed and be still. Offer the sacrifices of righteousness and put your trust in the Lord. here be many that say, who will shew us any good? Lord, lift thou up the light of thy countenance upon us. Thou hast put gladness in my heart, more than in the time that their corn and their wine increased. I will both lay me down in peace, and sleep: For You alone, O Lord, make me dwell in safety and confident trust."

- Psalm 4:4-8

Day Seventeen: Rest & Recovery.

Dear Lord, I humbly beg You, through the intercession of St Josemaría Escrivá, Your humble and faithful servant, for the grace to find peace and rest in Your most Holy Presence. When there is little time for leisure, may I always find time for recovery with You dearest Lord, Jesus. May I also make time for healing and solitude in meditation with Our Lady by praying the Holy Rosary. It is this devotion which gives me strength so that I may continue to serve You and walk the Way of The Cross.

Prayer to St Josemaría Escrivá

Most loving God, through the mediation of Our Lady, the Blessed Virgin, You chose St Josemaría Escrivá to serve You and honour you. You have gifted St Josemaría Escrivá the wisdom and grace to form Opus Dei, a way of sanctification in daily work and in the fulfilment of the Christian's ordinary life and duties. Grant that I too may learn to turn my everyday life into one that serves You God, and imitates the way of St Josemaría Escrivá with a zeal for loving all souls and striving for sanctification. Grant unto me God, through the intercession of St Josemaría Escrivá the favour of (intention).

Day Seventeen: Rest & Recovery.

"Do not be anxious about anything, but in everything by prayer and supplication with thanksgiving let your requests be made known to God. And the peace of God, which surpasses all understanding, will guard your hearts and your minds in Christ Jesus."

- Philippians 4:6-7

Holy Rosary of Joyful Mysteries

I believe in God, the Father Almighty, Creator of Heaven, and earth; and in Jesus Christ, His only Son, Our Lord, who was conceived by the Holy Ghost, born of the Virgin Mary, suffered under Pontius Pilate, was crucified; died, and was buried. He descended into Hell; the third day He arose again from the dead; He ascended into Heaven, sitteth at the right hand of God, the Father Almighty; from thence He shall come to judge the living and the dead. I believe in the Holy Spirit, the holy Catholic Church, the communion of saints, the forgiveness of sins, the resurrection of the body, and life everlasting.

Our Father, who art in heaven, hallowed be Thy name; Thy kingdom come; Thy will be done on earth as it is in heaven. Give us this day our daily bread; and forgive us our trespasses as we forgive those who trespass against us; and lead us not into temptation, but deliver us from evil.

Hail Mary, full of grace. The Lord is with thee. Blessed art thou among women, and blessed is the fruit of thy womb, Jesus. Holy Mary, Mother of God, pray for us sinners, now and at the hour of our death.

Glory be to the Father, to the Son, and to the Holy Spirit, as it was, is now, and ever shall be, world without end. Amen.

The Five Joyful Mysteries are prayed Monday and Saturday.

The Joyful Mysteries remind the faithful of Our Lady's Fiat and Christ's birth:

The Annunciation (Luke 1:26–38); The Visitation (Luke 1:39–56) The Nativity (Luke 2:1–21); The Presentation (Luke 2:22–38) The Finding of the Child Jesus in the Temple (Luke 2:41–52)

Hail Holy Queen

Hail, Holy Queen, Mother of mercy, our life, our sweetness, and our hope. To thee do we cry, poor banished children of Eve, to thee do we send up our sighs, mourning and weeping in this vale of tears. Turn then, most gracious advocate, thine eyes of mercy toward us; and after this our exile show unto us the blessed fruit of thy womb Jesus, O clement, O loving, O sweet Virgin Mary.

Pray for us, O holy Mother of God. That we may be made worthy of the promises of Christ.

O God, whose only begotten Son, by His life, death, and resurrection, has purchased for us the rewards of eternal salvation; grant we beseech Thee, that meditating upon these mysteries of the most holy Rosary of the Blessed Virgin Mary, we may imitate what they contain and obtain what they promise, through the same Christ our Lord.

Prayer to Our Lady of Guadalupe

Our Lady of Guadalupe, Mystical Rose, make intercession for the Holy Church, protect the Sovereign Pontiff, help all those who invoke thee in their necessities, and since thou art the Blessed Virgin Mary, and Mother of the True God, obtain for us from thy most holy Son the grace of keeping our faith, of sweet hope in the midst of the bitterness of life, of burning charity, and the most precious gift of perseverance so that we may carry our cross cheerfully.

St Josemaría Escrivá with students and members of Opus Dei at the University of Navarra, Spain.

Day Eighteen: Free Will.

"I defend with all my strength the freedom of consciences, which means that no one can licitly prevent a man from worshipping God. The legitimate hunger for truth must be respected. Man has a grave obligation to seek God, to know him and worship him, but no one on earth is permitted to impose on his neighbour the practice of a faith he lacks; just as no one can claim the right to harm those who have received the faith from God."

-St Josemaría Escrivá

Prayer Intention

Lord Jesus Christ, I desire to be a servant of Yours in accordance to the free will which God has gifted to myself and to all of humanity. Dear Lord, I know that I must respect and defend the freedom of conscience of those faithful to You. May You ignite within my spirit a fiery zeal to protect the freedom of religion and the right of every soul that wishes to seek Your most Holy Truth, always and forever.

"For if I preach the gospel, I have nothing to boast about, for this obligation has been entrusted to me. How terrible it would be for me if I didn't preach the gospel! For if I preach voluntarily, I get a reward, but if I am unwilling to do it, I am still entrusted with that obligation. What, then, is my reward? It is to be able to preach the gospel free of charge, and so I never resort to demanding my rights when I'm preaching the gospel. Although I am free from everyone's expectations, I have made myself a servant to all, to win more people.

- 1 Corinthians 9:16-19

Day Eighteen: Free Will.

Dear Lord, I humbly beg You, through the intercession of St Josemaría Escrivá, Your courageous and faithful servant, for the grace to give me courage too, so that I may proclaim the freedom which is true and not false. The false freedom which is licentious and selfish is to be rejected always in favour of the true freedom which can only be obtained by surrendering to the unconditional love which is You, Lord Jesus.

Prayer to St Josemaría Escrivá

Most loving God, through the mediation of Our Lady, the Blessed Virgin, You chose St Josemaría Escrivá to serve You and honour you. You have gifted St Josemaría Escrivá the wisdom and grace to form Opus Dei, a way of sanctification in daily work and in the fulfilment of the Christian's ordinary life and duties. Grant that I too may learn to turn my everyday life into one that serves You God, and imitates the way of St Josemaría Escrivá with a zeal for loving all souls and striving for sanctification. Grant unto me God, through the intercession of St Josemaría Escrivá the favour of (intention).

Day Eighteen: Free Will.

"But now that you have been set free from sin and have become slaves of God, the fruit you get leads to sanctification and its end, eternal life."

- Romans 6:22

Holy Rosary of Sorrowful Mysteries

I believe in God, the Father Almighty, Creator of Heaven, and earth; and in Jesus Christ, His only Son, Our Lord, who was conceived by the Holy Ghost, born of the Virgin Mary, suffered under Pontius Pilate, was crucified; died, and was buried. He descended into Hell; the third day He arose again from the dead; He ascended into Heaven, sitteth at the right hand of God, the Father Almighty; from thence He shall come to judge the living and the dead. I believe in the Holy Spirit, the holy Catholic Church, the communion of saints, the forgiveness of sins, the resurrection of the body, and life everlasting.

Our Father, who art in heaven, hallowed be Thy name; Thy kingdom come; Thy will be done on earth as it is in heaven. Give us this day our daily bread; and forgive us our trespasses as we forgive those who trespass against us; and lead us not into temptation, but deliver us from evil.

Hail Mary, full of grace. The Lord is with thee. Blessed art thou among women, and blessed is the fruit of thy womb, Jesus. Holy Mary, Mother of God, pray for us sinners, now and at the hour of our death.

Glory be to the Father, to the Son, and to the Holy Spirit, as it was, is now, and ever shall be, world without end. Amen.

The Five Sorrowful Mysteries are prayed Tuesday and Friday.

The Sorrowful Mysteries remind the faithful of Christ's Passion and of His Crucifixion:

The Agony of Jesus in the Garden (Matthew 26:36–56); The Scourging at the Pillar (Matthew 27:26) The Crowning with Thorns (Matthew 27:27–31); The Carrying of the Cross (Matthew 27:32) The Crucifixion (Matthew 27:33–56)

Hail Holy Queen

Hail, Holy Queen, Mother of mercy, our life, our sweetness, and our hope. To thee do we cry, poor banished children of Eve, to thee do we send up our sighs, mourning and weeping in this vale of tears. Turn then, most gracious advocate, thine eyes of mercy toward us; and after this our exile show unto us the blessed fruit of thy womb Jesus, O clement, O loving, O sweet Virgin Mary.

Pray for us, O holy Mother of God. That we may be made worthy of the promises of Christ.

O God, whose only begotten Son, by His life, death, and resurrection, has purchased for us the rewards of eternal salvation; grant we beseech Thee, that meditating upon these mysteries of the most holy Rosary of the Blessed Virgin Mary, we may imitate what they contain and obtain what they promise, through the same Christ our Lord.

Prayer to Our Lady of Guadalupe

Our Lady of Guadalupe, Mystical Rose, make intercession for the Holy Church, protect the Sovereign Pontiff, help all those who invoke thee in their necessities, and since thou art the Blessed Virgin Mary, and Mother of the True God, obtain for us from thy most holy Son the grace of keeping our faith, of sweet hope in the midst of the bitterness of life, of burning charity, and the most precious gift of perseverance so that we may carry our cross cheerfully.

St Josemaría Escrivá at the Grotto of Our Lady of Lourdes in 1960.

Day Nineteen: Simplicity.

"Nowhere is it written that Christians should be strangers to the world. Our Lord Jesus by his deeds and by his teaching has bestowed praise on another human virtue which is particularly dear to me, the virtue of naturalness or simplicity. Remember how Our Lord comes into the world, just like every other human being. He spends his childhood and adolescence in a village in Palestine, where he is no different from his fellow villagers."

-St Josemaría Escrivá

Prayer Intention

Lord Jesus Christ, I desire to have a spirit of simplicity. How simple and clean the rainfall is, and how simple yet beautiful the blooming of spring flowers. They do not stand out, indeed many of us take for granted the rain and even find annoyance at the showers, which, with each drop nourishes the planted seeds so that they may grow and bear good fruit. It is just the same, that without You dear Lord, we cannot bear good fruit which is spiritually nourishing. I pray that all planted seeds of faith flourish and blossom.

"Then called I upon the name of the Lord; O LORD, I beseech thee, deliver my soul. Gracious is the Lord, and righteous; Yes, our God is compassionate. The Lord preserves the simple; when I was brought low, he saved me. Return unto thy rest, O my soul; for the LORD hath dealt bountifully with thee."

- Psalm 116:4-7

Day Nineteen: Simplicity.

Dear Lord, I humbly beg You, through the intercession of St Josemaría Escrivá, for the wisdom and grace to live my life each day with simplicity in accordance to Your will. I ask that You keep me from falling into the snares of the wicked one who is evil by way of sowing seeds of discord, confusion and causes the intellectual mind of the believer to question and ponder upon which is unnecessary, instead of simply trusting in You fully, with the pure unadulterated mind and spirit of a child.

Prayer to St Josemaría Escrivá

Most loving God, through the mediation of Our Lady, the Blessed Virgin, You chose St Josemaría Escrivá to serve You and honour you. You have gifted St Josemaría Escrivá the wisdom and grace to form Opus Dei, a way of sanctification in daily work and in the fulfilment of the Christian's ordinary life and duties. Grant that I too may learn to turn my everyday life into one that serves You God, and imitates the way of St Josemaría Escrivá with a zeal for loving all souls and striving for sanctification. Grant unto me God, through the intercession of St Josemaría Escrivá the favour of (intention).

Day Nineteen: Simplicity.

"In that same hour he rejoiced in the Holy Spirit and said, "I thank you, Father, Lord of heaven and earth, that you have hidden these things from the wise and understanding and revealed them to little children; yes, Father, for such was your gracious will."

- Luke 10:21

Holy Rosary of Glorious Mysteries

I believe in God, the Father Almighty, Creator of Heaven, and earth; and in Jesus Christ, His only Son, Our Lord, who was conceived by the Holy Ghost, born of the Virgin Mary, suffered under Pontius Pilate, was crucified; died, and was buried. He descended into Hell; the third day He arose again from the dead; He ascended into Heaven, sitteth at the right hand of God, the Father Almighty; from thence He shall come to judge the living and the dead. I believe in the Holy Spirit, the holy Catholic Church, the communion of saints, the forgiveness of sins, the resurrection of the body, and life everlasting.

Our Father, who art in heaven, hallowed be Thy name; Thy kingdom come; Thy will be done on earth as it is in heaven. Give us this day our daily bread; and forgive us our trespasses as we forgive those who trespass against us; and lead us not into temptation, but deliver us from evil.

Hail Mary, full of grace. The Lord is with thee. Blessed art thou among women, and blessed is the fruit of thy womb, Jesus. Holy Mary, Mother of God, pray for us sinners, now and at the hour of our death.

Glory be to the Father, to the Son, and to the Holy Spirit, as it was, is now, and ever shall be, world without end. Amen.

The Five Glorious Mysteries are prayed Wednesday and Sunday.

The Glorious Mysteries remind the faithful of Christ's Resurrection and Heaven's glories:

The Resurrection (Luke 24:1-12); The Ascension (Acts 1:6-11) The Descent of the Holy Spirit (Acts 2:1-4); The Assumption (Munificentissimus Deus 44) The Coronation of Mary as Queen of Heaven (Revelations 12:1-6)

Hail Holy Queen

Hail, Holy Queen, Mother of mercy, our life, our sweetness, and our hope. To thee do we cry, poor banished children of Eve, to thee do we send up our sighs, mourning and weeping in this vale of tears. Turn then, most gracious advocate, thine eyes of mercy toward us; and after this our exile show unto us the blessed fruit of thy womb Jesus, O clement, O loving, O sweet Virgin Mary.

Pray for us, O holy Mother of God. That we may be made worthy of the promises of Christ.

O God, whose only begotten Son, by His life, death, and resurrection, has purchased for us the rewards of eternal salvation; grant we beseech Thee, that meditating upon these mysteries of the most holy Rosary of the Blessed Virgin Mary, we may imitate what they contain and obtain what they promise, through the same Christ our Lord.

Prayer to Our Lady of Guadalupe

Our Lady of Guadalupe, Mystical Rose, make intercession for the Holy Church, protect the Sovereign Pontiff, help all those who invoke thee in their necessities, and since thou art the Blessed Virgin Mary, and Mother of the True God, obtain for us from thy most holy Son the grace of keeping our faith, of sweet hope in the midst of the bitterness of life, of burning charity, and the most precious gift of perseverance so that we may carry our cross cheerfully.

St Josemaría Escrivá and Blessed Alvaro del Portillo with
St Pope John XXII in 1960.

Day Twenty: Providence.

"People are doing various things and all think they are right. But God is guiding them, that is to say, over and above their own particular ideas, God's inscrutable and most lovable Providence will win through in the end. Allow yourself, therefore, to be guided by the Lord, without opposing His plans, even though they might go against your basic assumptions."

-St Josemaría Escrivá

Prayer Intention

Lord Jesus Christ, I desire to detach from that within me which is the ego and voice of pride which may blind me from seeing Your most holy will make itself known to me. I ask that You bestow upon me a heart filled with humility and a spirit full of wonder so that I do not miss the many gifts and opportunities which You present to me as indiscreet blessings in my life, by Your divine providence.

"So, we have the prophetic word made surer, to which you do well to pay attention as to a lamp shining in a dark place, until the day dawns and the morning star arises in your hearts. But know this first of all; that no prophecy of Scripture is a matter of one's own interpretation, no prophecy was ever produced by the will of man, but men spoke from God as they were carried along by the Holy Spirit."

- 2 Peter 1:19-21

Day Twenty: Providence.

Dear Lord, I humbly beg You, through the intercession of St Josemaría Escrivá, for the grace to live my life each day with virtue and faith in Your most holy Presence. May my eyes be open to You, my heart be overflowing with love for You, and my spirit be willing and accepting of letting You take control and lead me down the path of righteousness through Your providence.

Prayer to St Josemaría Escrivá

Most loving God, through the mediation of Our Lady, the Blessed Virgin, You chose St Josemaría Escrivá to serve You and honour you. You have gifted St Josemaría Escrivá the wisdom and grace to form Opus Dei, a way of sanctification in daily work and in the fulfilment of the Christian's ordinary life and duties. Grant that I too may learn to turn my everyday life into one that serves You God, and imitates the way of St Josemaría Escrivá with a zeal for loving all souls and striving for sanctification. Grant unto me God, through the intercession of St Josemaría Escrivá the favour of (intention).

Day Twenty: Providence.

"For I know the plans I have for you, declares the Lord, plans for welfare and not for evil, to give you a future and a hope."

- Jeremiah 29:11

Holy Rosary of Luminous Mysteries

I believe in God, the Father Almighty, Creator of Heaven, and earth; and in Jesus Christ, His only Son, Our Lord, who was conceived by the Holy Ghost, born of the Virgin Mary, suffered under Pontius Pilate, was crucified; died, and was buried. He descended into Hell; the third day He arose again from the dead; He ascended into Heaven, sitteth at the right hand of God, the Father Almighty; from thence He shall come to judge the living and the dead. I believe in the Holy Spirit, the holy Catholic Church, the communion of saints, the forgiveness of sins, the resurrection of the body, and life everlasting.

Our Father, who art in heaven, hallowed be Thy name; Thy kingdom come; Thy will be done on earth as it is in heaven. Give us this day our daily bread; and forgive us our trespasses as we forgive those who trespass against us; and lead us not into temptation, but deliver us from evil.

Hail Mary, full of grace. The Lord is with thee. Blessed art thou among women, and blessed is the fruit of thy womb, Jesus. Holy Mary, Mother of God, pray for us sinners, now and at the hour of our death.

Glory be to the Father, to the Son, and to the Holy Spirit, as it was, is now, and ever shall be, world without end. Amen.

The Five Luminous Mysteries are prayed on Thursday.

The Luminous Mysteries remind the faithful of Christ's shining light:

The Baptism in the River Jordan (Matthew 3:13–16); The Wedding Feast at Cana (John 2:1–11) The Preaching of the coming of the Kingdom of God (Mark 1:14–15) The Transfiguration (Matthew 17:1–8); The Institution of the Holy Eucharist (Matthew 26)

Hail Holy Queen

Hail, Holy Queen, Mother of mercy, our life, our sweetness, and our hope. To thee do we cry, poor banished children of Eve, to thee do we send up our sighs, mourning and weeping in this vale of tears. Turn then, most gracious advocate, thine eyes of mercy toward us; and after this our exile show unto us the blessed fruit of thy womb Jesus, O clement, O loving, O sweet Virgin Mary.

Pray for us, O holy Mother of God. That we may be made worthy of the promises of Christ.

O God, whose only begotten Son, by His life, death, and resurrection, has purchased for us the rewards of eternal salvation; grant we beseech Thee, that meditating upon these mysteries of the most holy Rosary of the Blessed Virgin Mary, we may imitate what they contain and obtain what they promise, through the same Christ our Lord.

Prayer to Our Lady of Guadalupe

Our Lady of Guadalupe, Mystical Rose, make intercession for the Holy Church, protect the Sovereign Pontiff, help all those who invoke thee in their necessities, and since thou art the Blessed Virgin Mary, and Mother of the True God, obtain for us from thy most holy Son the grace of keeping our faith, of sweet hope in the midst of the bitterness of life, of burning charity, and the most precious gift of perseverance so that we may carry our cross cheerfully.

St Josemaría Escrivá with St Pope Paul IV in 1965.

Day Twenty-One: Natural Law.

"I tell you once again: I accept no slavery other than that of God's Love. This is because, as I have told you on other occasions, religion is the greatest rebellion of men, who refuse to live like animals, who are dissatisfied and restless until they know their Creator and are on intimate terms with Him."

-St Josemaría Escrivá

Prayer Intention

Lord Jesus Christ, I desire to live my life in accordance to the natural law which You proclaim. I exist because You have created me in Your image, dear Lord. There need not be anything artificial or fabricated about the way in which I live my life in accordance to Your most holy will. What comes natural to me is love for You, my Lord and my God, who has sacrificed Himself for my redemption. Only You, Dear Lord are the Truth in this world. Your love for me radiates from the Eucharist, in which Your True Presence is known.

"For the wrath of God is revealed from heaven against all ungodliness and unrighteousness of men, who hold the truth in unrighteousness; Because that which may be known of God is manifest in them; for God hath shewed it unto them. For the invisible things of him from the creation of the world are clearly seen, being understood by the things that are made, even his eternal power and Godhead; so that they are without excuse: For though they knew God, they did not glorify Him as God or show gratitude. Instead, their thinking became nonsense, and their senseless minds were darkened."

- Romans 1:18-21

Day Twenty-One: Natural Law.

Dear Lord, I humbly beg You, through the intercession of St Josemaría Escrivá, for the grace to fill my spirit with a natural fervour towards all that is holy and good so that I may live my life each day faithfully. I ask that You fill my heart with enthusiasm so that I may, naturally, through Your wisdom, lead souls closer to Your most loving Sacred Heart. May You guide me always to help those seeking refuge to find it in You.

Prayer to St Josemaría Escrivá

Most loving God, through the mediation of Our Lady, the Blessed Virgin, You chose St Josemaría Escrivá to serve You and honour you. You have gifted St Josemaría Escrivá the wisdom and grace to form Opus Dei, a way of sanctification in daily work and in the fulfilment of the Christian's ordinary life and duties. Grant that I too may learn to turn my everyday life into one that serves You God, and imitates the way of St Josemaría Escrivá with a zeal for loving all souls and striving for sanctification. Grant unto me God, through the intercession of St Josemaría Escrivá the favour of (intention).

Day Twenty-One: Natural Law.

"For the law was given through Moses; grace and truth came through Jesus Christ."

- John 1:17

Holy Rosary of Joyful Mysteries

I believe in God, the Father Almighty, Creator of Heaven, and earth; and in Jesus Christ, His only Son, Our Lord, who was conceived by the Holy Ghost, born of the Virgin Mary, suffered under Pontius Pilate, was crucified; died, and was buried. He descended into Hell; the third day He arose again from the dead; He ascended into Heaven, sitteth at the right hand of God, the Father Almighty; from thence He shall come to judge the living and the dead. I believe in the Holy Spirit, the holy Catholic Church, the communion of saints, the forgiveness of sins, the resurrection of the body, and life everlasting.

Our Father, who art in heaven, hallowed be Thy name; Thy kingdom come; Thy will be done on earth as it is in heaven. Give us this day our daily bread; and forgive us our trespasses as we forgive those who trespass against us; and lead us not into temptation, but deliver us from evil.

Hail Mary, full of grace. The Lord is with thee. Blessed art thou among women, and blessed is the fruit of thy womb, Jesus. Holy Mary, Mother of God, pray for us sinners, now and at the hour of our death.

Glory be to the Father, to the Son, and to the Holy Spirit, as it was, is now, and ever shall be, world without end. Amen.

The Five Joyful Mysteries are prayed Monday and Saturday.

The Joyful Mysteries remind the faithful of Our Lady's Fiat and Christ's birth:

The Annunciation (Luke 1:26–38); The Visitation (Luke 1:39–56) The Nativity (Luke 2:1–21); The Presentation (Luke 2:22–38) The Finding of the Child Jesus in the Temple (Luke 2:41–52)

Hail Holy Queen

Hail, Holy Queen, Mother of mercy, our life, our sweetness, and our hope. To thee do we cry, poor banished children of Eve, to thee do we send up our sighs, mourning and weeping in this vale of tears. Turn then, most gracious advocate, thine eyes of mercy toward us; and after this our exile show unto us the blessed fruit of thy womb Jesus, O clement, O loving, O sweet Virgin Mary.

Pray for us, O holy Mother of God. That we may be made worthy of the promises of Christ.

O God, whose only begotten Son, by His life, death, and resurrection, has purchased for us the rewards of eternal salvation; grant we beseech Thee, that meditating upon these mysteries of the most holy Rosary of the Blessed Virgin Mary, we may imitate what they contain and obtain what they promise, through the same Christ our Lord.

Prayer to Our Lady of Guadalupe

Our Lady of Guadalupe, Mystical Rose, make intercession for the Holy Church, protect the Sovereign Pontiff, help all those who invoke thee in their necessities, and since thou art the Blessed Virgin Mary, and Mother of the True God, obtain for us from thy most holy Son the grace of keeping our faith, of sweet hope in the midst of the bitterness of life, of burning charity, and the most precious gift of perseverance so that we may carry our cross cheerfully.

St Josemaría Escrivá in 1968.

Day Twenty-Two: Maturity.

"Our Lord has said: "Unless you become like little children, you will not enter the kingdom of heaven." This is the old and well-known "way of childhood" which is not sentimentality or lack of human maturity. It is a supernatural maturity, which makes us realize more deeply the wonders of God's love, while leading us to acknowledge our own smallness and identify our will fully with God's will."

-St Josemaría Escrivá

Prayer Intention

Lord Jesus Christ, I desire to have the faith of a small child who finds shelter in Your most loving Sacred Heart. Like a child who trusts and loves You unconditionally, I aspire to open my heart and my mind fully to Your most holy will, dear Lord. I stand before the Eucharist, a small child in Your eyes, with enthusiasm for the faith, loving You, my Heavenly Father. I put all of my trust in You, dear Jesus Christ.

"Like newborn infants, long for the pure spiritual milk, that by it you may grow up into salvation if you have tasted the kindness of the Lord. To whom coming, as unto a living stone, disallowed indeed of men, but chosen of God, and precious, you yourselves, as living stones, are being built into a spiritual house for a holy priesthood to offer spiritual sacrifices acceptable to God through Jesus Christ. Therefore, it says in Scripture: "Look! I am laying a chosen, precious cornerstone in Zion. The one who believes in him will never be ashamed."

- 1 Peter 2:2-6

Day Twenty-Two: Maturity.

Dear Lord, I humbly beg You, through the intercession of St Josemaría Escrivá, for the grace to fill my spirit with a childlike faith and to allow me to fully trust in You as You guide me along the path of righteousness so that I may attain sainthood. I know that I must always cherish and trust in those whom You have appointed as modern apostles. The many priests, and bishops of Your one Holy Apostolic Church, represent You as the Father, in whom I must listen to carefully and humbly submit to, with obedience and love.

Prayer to St Josemaría Escrivá

Most loving God, through the mediation of Our Lady, the Blessed Virgin, You chose St Josemaría Escrivá to serve You and honour you. You have gifted St Josemaría Escrivá the wisdom and grace to form Opus Dei, a way of sanctification in daily work and in the fulfilment of the Christian's ordinary life and duties. Grant that I too may learn to turn my everyday life into one that serves You God, and imitates the way of St Josemaría Escrivá with a zeal for loving all souls and striving for sanctification. Grant unto me God, through the intercession of St Josemaría Escrivá the favour of (intention).

Day Twenty-Two: Maturity.

"But grow in the grace and knowledge of our Lord and Saviour Jesus Christ. To him be the glory both now and to the day of eternity. Amen."

- 2 Peter 3:18

Holy Rosary of Sorrowful Mysteries

I believe in God, the Father Almighty, Creator of Heaven, and earth; and in Jesus Christ, His only Son, Our Lord, who was conceived by the Holy Ghost, born of the Virgin Mary, suffered under Pontius Pilate, was crucified; died, and was buried. He descended into Hell; the third day He arose again from the dead; He ascended into Heaven, sitteth at the right hand of God, the Father Almighty; from thence He shall come to judge the living and the dead. I believe in the Holy Spirit, the holy Catholic Church, the communion of saints, the forgiveness of sins, the resurrection of the body, and life everlasting.

Our Father, who art in heaven, hallowed be Thy name; Thy kingdom come; Thy will be done on earth as it is in heaven. Give us this day our daily bread; and forgive us our trespasses as we forgive those who trespass against us; and lead us not into temptation, but deliver us from evil.

Hail Mary, full of grace. The Lord is with thee. Blessed art thou among women, and blessed is the fruit of thy womb, Jesus. Holy Mary, Mother of God, pray for us sinners, now and at the hour of our death.

Glory be to the Father, to the Son, and to the Holy Spirit, as it was, is now, and ever shall be, world without end. Amen.

The Five Sorrowful Mysteries are prayed Tuesday and Friday.

The Sorrowful Mysteries remind the faithful of Christ's Passion and of His Crucifixion:

The Agony of Jesus in the Garden (Matthew 26:36–56); The Scourging at the Pillar (Matthew 27:26) The Crowning with Thorns (Matthew 27:27–31); The Carrying of the Cross (Matthew 27:32) The Crucifixion (Matthew 27:33–56)

Hail Holy Queen

Hail, Holy Queen, Mother of mercy, our life, our sweetness, and our hope. To thee do we cry, poor banished children of Eve, to thee do we send up our sighs, mourning and weeping in this vale of tears. Turn then, most gracious advocate, thine eyes of mercy toward us; and after this our exile show unto us the blessed fruit of thy womb Jesus, O clement, O loving, O sweet Virgin Mary.

Pray for us, O holy Mother of God. That we may be made worthy of the promises of Christ.

O God, whose only begotten Son, by His life, death, and resurrection, has purchased for us the rewards of eternal salvation; grant we beseech Thee, that meditating upon these mysteries of the most holy Rosary of the Blessed Virgin Mary, we may imitate what they contain and obtain what they promise, through the same Christ our Lord.

Prayer to Our Lady of Guadalupe

Our Lady of Guadalupe, Mystical Rose, make intercession for the Holy Church, protect the Sovereign Pontiff, help all those who invoke thee in their necessities, and since thou art the Blessed Virgin Mary, and Mother of the True God, obtain for us from thy most holy Son the grace of keeping our faith, of sweet hope in the midst of the bitterness of life, of burning charity, and the most precious gift of perseverance so that we may carry our cross cheerfully.

St Josemaría Escrivá with members of Opus Dei in 1970.

Day Twenty-Three: The Holy Rosary.

"The Holy Rosary: the joys, the sorrows, and the glories of the life of Our Lady weave a crown of praises, repeated ceaselessly by the Angels and the Saints in Heaven and by those who love our Mother here on earth. Practise this holy devotion every day and spread it."

-St Josemaría Escrivá

Prayer Intention

Lord Jesus Christ, desire to pray and meditate on the Holy Rosary each and every day so that I may grow closer to You through the intercession of Our Lady. I know that I can do this faithfully with routine and Marian devotion. I aspired to dedicate time each day, to pray the Holy Rosary for the souls in purgatory, and for those who are suffering and in need of Our Lady's most comforting Motherly love. Our Lady, is the ever so loving and through her, may we find solace in You, dear Lord.

"The prayer of faith will save the sick person, and the Lord will restore him to health; if he has committed sins, he will be forgiven. Therefore, confess your sins to one another and pray for one another, that you may be healed. The prayer of a righteous person has great power as it is working. Elijah was a man with a nature like ours; yet he prayed earnestly that it would not rain, and for three years and six months it did not rain on the land. Then he prayed again, and the sky gave rain, and the land produced its fruit."

- James 5:15-18

Day Twenty-Three: The Holy Rosary.

Dear Lord, I humbly beg You, through the intercession of St Josemaría Escrivá, for the grace to fill my spirit with enthusiasm and zeal for prayer. Our Lady in heaven, awaits us with a mother's patience and compassion. Dear Lord, please give me the fortitude to pray the Holy Rosary each and every day, and to pray it with passion, for each bead is a steppingstone towards deeper devotion and love for Our Lady.

Prayer to St Josemaría Escrivá

Most loving God, through the mediation of Our Lady, the Blessed Virgin, You chose St Josemaría Escrivá to serve You and honour you. You have gifted St Josemaría Escrivá the wisdom and grace to form Opus Dei, a way of sanctification in daily work and in the fulfilment of the Christian's ordinary life and duties. Grant that I too may learn to turn my everyday life into one that serves You God, and imitates the way of St Josemaría Escrivá with a zeal for loving all souls and striving for sanctification. Grant unto me God, through the intercession of St Josemaría Escrivá the favour of (intention).

Day Twenty-Three: The Holy Rosary.

"And rising very early in the morning, while it was still dark, he departed and went out to a desolate place, and there he prayed."

- Mark 1:35

Holy Rosary of Glorious Mysteries

I believe in God, the Father Almighty, Creator of Heaven, and earth; and in Jesus Christ, His only Son, Our Lord, who was conceived by the Holy Ghost, born of the Virgin Mary, suffered under Pontius Pilate, was crucified; died, and was buried. He descended into Hell; the third day He arose again from the dead; He ascended into Heaven, sitteth at the right hand of God, the Father Almighty; from thence He shall come to judge the living and the dead. I believe in the Holy Spirit, the holy Catholic Church, the communion of saints, the forgiveness of sins, the resurrection of the body, and life everlasting.

Our Father, who art in heaven, hallowed be Thy name; Thy kingdom come; Thy will be done on earth as it is in heaven. Give us this day our daily bread; and forgive us our trespasses as we forgive those who trespass against us; and lead us not into temptation, but deliver us from evil.

Hail Mary, full of grace. The Lord is with thee. Blessed art thou among women, and blessed is the fruit of thy womb, Jesus. Holy Mary, Mother of God, pray for us sinners, now and at the hour of our death.

Glory be to the Father, to the Son, and to the Holy Spirit, as it was, is now, and ever shall be, world without end. Amen.

The Five Glorious Mysteries are prayed Wednesday and Sunday.

The Glorious Mysteries remind the faithful of Christ's Resurrection and Heaven's glories:

The Resurrection (Luke 24:1-12); The Ascension (Acts 1:6-11) The Descent of the Holy Spirit (Acts 2:1-4); The Assumption (Munificentissimus Deus 44) The Coronation of Mary as Queen of Heaven (Revelations 12:1-6)

Hail Holy Queen

Hail, Holy Queen, Mother of mercy, our life, our sweetness, and our hope. To thee do we cry, poor banished children of Eve, to thee do we send up our sighs, mourning and weeping in this vale of tears. Turn then, most gracious advocate, thine eyes of mercy toward us; and after this our exile show unto us the blessed fruit of thy womb Jesus, O clement, O loving, O sweet Virgin Mary.

Pray for us, O holy Mother of God. That we may be made worthy of the promises of Christ.

O God, whose only begotten Son, by His life, death, and resurrection, has purchased for us the rewards of eternal salvation; grant we beseech Thee, that meditating upon these mysteries of the most holy Rosary of the Blessed Virgin Mary, we may imitate what they contain and obtain what they promise, through the same Christ our Lord.

Prayer to Our Lady of Guadalupe

Our Lady of Guadalupe, Mystical Rose, make intercession for the Holy Church, protect the Sovereign Pontiff, help all those who invoke thee in their necessities, and since thou art the Blessed Virgin Mary, and Mother of the True God, obtain for us from thy most holy Son the grace of keeping our faith, of sweet hope in the midst of the bitterness of life, of burning charity, and the most precious gift of perseverance so that we may carry our cross cheerfully.

St Josemaría Escrivá praying the Holy Rosary.

Day Twenty-Four: Conscience.

"Examine your conscience sincerely: perhaps neither you nor I deserve the praise that country priest had for his donkey. We have worked so hard, held responsible positions, you have won success in men's eyes in such and such a job... But, in God's presence, is there nothing you regret? Have you truly tried to serve God and your fellow men? Or have you pursued your own selfish plans, your personal glory, your own ambitions, seeking a purely earthly success that will dwindle pitifully into nothingness?"

-St Josemaría Escrivá

Prayer Intention

Lord Jesus Christ, I desire to contemplate more on You, improve my life and the life of others through Your guidance and Your word. I must examine my conscience thoroughly and rectify the errors of my ways. I ask of You, dear Lord, to instil into my heart, a fiery passion for the faith, so that I may humble myself in Your presence, and not judge others so harshly, for I am myself, a sinner in need of Your infinite mercy.

"This is a trustworthy saying that deserves complete acceptance: To this world Messiah came, sinful people to reclaim. I am the worst of them. But for that very reason I received mercy, so that in me, as the worst sinner, the Messiah Jesus might demonstrate all of his patience as an example for those who would believe in him for eternal life.

- 1 Timothy 1:15-16

Day Twenty-Four: Conscience.

Dear Lord, I humbly beg You, through the intercession of St Josemaría Escrivá, for the grace to fill my spirit with humility so that I may examine my conscience thoroughly and make a good confession. It is through introspection, and devotion to leading a fruitful Christian life, that I must grow to examine my faults. It is through my sin that You are crucified, dear Lord. Mea culpa, Mea maxima culpa.

Prayer to St Josemaría Escrivá

Most loving God, through the mediation of Our Lady, the Blessed Virgin, You chose St Josemaría Escrivá to serve You and honour you. You have gifted St Josemaría Escrivá the wisdom and grace to form Opus Dei, a way of sanctification in daily work and in the fulfilment of the Christian's ordinary life and duties. Grant that I too may learn to turn my everyday life into one that serves You God, and imitates the way of St Josemaría Escrivá with a zeal for loving all souls and striving for sanctification. Grant unto me God, through the intercession of St Josemaría Escrivá the favour of (intention).

Day Twenty-Four: Conscience.

"Having a good conscience, so that when you are slandered, those who revile your good behaviour in Christ may be put to shame."

- 1 Peter 3:16

Holy Rosary of Luminous Mysteries

I believe in God, the Father Almighty, Creator of Heaven, and earth; and in Jesus Christ, His only Son, Our Lord, who was conceived by the Holy Ghost, born of the Virgin Mary, suffered under Pontius Pilate, was crucified; died, and was buried. He descended into Hell; the third day He arose again from the dead; He ascended into Heaven, sitteth at the right hand of God, the Father Almighty; from thence He shall come to judge the living and the dead. I believe in the Holy Spirit, the holy Catholic Church, the communion of saints, the forgiveness of sins, the resurrection of the body, and life everlasting.

Our Father, who art in heaven, hallowed be Thy name; Thy kingdom come; Thy will be done on earth as it is in heaven. Give us this day our daily bread; and forgive us our trespasses as we forgive those who trespass against us; and lead us not into temptation, but deliver us from evil.

Hail Mary, full of grace. The Lord is with thee. Blessed art thou among women, and blessed is the fruit of thy womb, Jesus. Holy Mary, Mother of God, pray for us sinners, now and at the hour of our death.

Glory be to the Father, to the Son, and to the Holy Spirit, as it was, is now, and ever shall be, world without end. Amen.

The Five Luminous Mysteries are prayed on Thursday.

The Luminous Mysteries remind the faithful of Christ's shining light:

The Baptism in the River Jordan (Matthew 3:13–16); The Wedding Feast at Cana (John 2:1–11) The Preaching of the coming of the Kingdom of God (Mark 1:14–15) The Transfiguration (Matthew 17:1–8); The Institution of the Holy Eucharist (Matthew 26)

Hail Holy Queen

Hail, Holy Queen, Mother of mercy, our life, our sweetness, and our hope. To thee do we cry, poor banished children of Eve, to thee do we send up our sighs, mourning and weeping in this vale of tears. Turn then, most gracious advocate, thine eyes of mercy toward us; and after this our exile show unto us the blessed fruit of thy womb Jesus, O clement, O loving, O sweet Virgin Mary.

Pray for us, O holy Mother of God. That we may be made worthy of the promises of Christ.

O God, whose only begotten Son, by His life, death, and resurrection, has purchased for us the rewards of eternal salvation; grant we beseech Thee, that meditating upon these mysteries of the most holy Rosary of the Blessed Virgin Mary, we may imitate what they contain and obtain what they promise, through the same Christ our Lord.

Prayer to Our Lady of Guadalupe

Our Lady of Guadalupe, Mystical Rose, make intercession for the Holy Church, protect the Sovereign Pontiff, help all those who invoke thee in their necessities, and since thou art the Blessed Virgin Mary, and Mother of the True God, obtain for us from thy most holy Son the grace of keeping our faith, of sweet hope in the midst of the bitterness of life, of burning charity, and the most precious gift of perseverance so that we may carry our cross cheerfully.

St Josemaría Escrivá speaks to members of Opus Dei in 1970.

Day Twenty-Five: Prudence.

"Such wisdom of the heart, such prudence will never become the prudence of the flesh that St Paul speaks of, the prudence of those who are intelligent but try not to use their intelligence to seek and love Our Lord. A truly prudent person is ever attentive to God's promptings, and, through this vigilant listening, he receives in his soul the promise and reality of salvation: I glorify Thee, Father, Lord of heaven and earth, for having hidden these things from the wise and prudent and revealed them to little ones."

-St Josemaría Escrivá

Prayer Intention

Lord Jesus Christ, I desire to exercise genuine prudence, which is not self-serving or cunning, but discerning and helps me to grow in my faith. Through attending the sacraments, Mass, and praying the Holy Rosary, I can learn to be more prudent and discerning so that I make the right choices which are focused on serving You and putting my trust in You, dear Lord.

"The simple believes everything, but the prudent gives thought to his steps. The wise person fears and turns away from evil, but a fool is reckless and overconfident. A quick-tempered person does foolish things, and a devious man is hated. The naive inherit folly, but the careful are crowned with knowledge."

- Proverbs 14:15-18

Day Twenty-Five: Prudence.

Dear Lord, I humbly beg You, through the intercession of St Josemaría Escrivá, for the grace to fill my spirit with prudence so that I may carefully discern each step I take down the path which You have laid out for me to follow. The path to Sainthood and sanctifying my every day ordinary life, is greatly enriched by exercising prudence, not being overindulgent or impulsive but by following You, Lord Jesus.

Prayer to St Josemaría Escrivá

Most loving God, through the mediation of Our Lady, the Blessed Virgin, You chose St Josemaría Escrivá to serve You and honour you. You have gifted St Josemaría Escrivá the wisdom and grace to form Opus Dei, a way of sanctification in daily work and in the fulfilment of the Christian's ordinary life and duties. Grant that I too may learn to turn my everyday life into one that serves You God, and imitates the way of St Josemaría Escrivá with a zeal for loving all souls and striving for sanctification. Grant unto me God, through the intercession of St Josemaría Escrivá the favour of (intention).

Day Twenty-Five: Prudence.

"When the Spirit of truth comes, he will guide you into all the truth, for he will not speak on his own authority, but whatever he hears he will speak, and he will declare to you the things that are to come."

- John 16:13

Holy Rosary of Joyful Mysteries

I believe in God, the Father Almighty, Creator of Heaven, and earth; and in Jesus Christ, His only Son, Our Lord, who was conceived by the Holy Ghost, born of the Virgin Mary, suffered under Pontius Pilate, was crucified; died, and was buried. He descended into Hell; the third day He arose again from the dead; He ascended into Heaven, sitteth at the right hand of God, the Father Almighty; from thence He shall come to judge the living and the dead. I believe in the Holy Spirit, the holy Catholic Church, the communion of saints, the forgiveness of sins, the resurrection of the body, and life everlasting.

Our Father, who art in heaven, hallowed be Thy name; Thy kingdom come; Thy will be done on earth as it is in heaven. Give us this day our daily bread; and forgive us our trespasses as we forgive those who trespass against us; and lead us not into temptation, but deliver us from evil.

Hail Mary, full of grace. The Lord is with thee. Blessed art thou among women, and blessed is the fruit of thy womb, Jesus. Holy Mary, Mother of God, pray for us sinners, now and at the hour of our death.

Glory be to the Father, to the Son, and to the Holy Spirit, as it was, is now, and ever shall be, world without end. Amen.

The Five Joyful Mysteries are prayed Monday and Saturday.

The Joyful Mysteries remind the faithful of Our Lady's Fiat and Christ's birth:

The Annunciation (Luke 1:26–38); The Visitation (Luke 1:39–56) The Nativity (Luke 2:1–21); The Presentation (Luke 2:22–38) The Finding of the Child Jesus in the Temple (Luke 2:41–52)

Hail Holy Queen

Hail, Holy Queen, Mother of mercy, our life, our sweetness, and our hope. To thee do we cry, poor banished children of Eve, to thee do we send up our sighs, mourning and weeping in this vale of tears. Turn then, most gracious advocate, thine eyes of mercy toward us; and after this our exile show unto us the blessed fruit of thy womb Jesus, O clement, O loving, O sweet Virgin Mary.

Pray for us, O holy Mother of God. That we may be made worthy of the promises of Christ.

O God, whose only begotten Son, by His life, death, and resurrection, has purchased for us the rewards of eternal salvation; grant we beseech Thee, that meditating upon these mysteries of the most holy Rosary of the Blessed Virgin Mary, we may imitate what they contain and obtain what they promise, through the same Christ our Lord.

Prayer to Our Lady of Guadalupe

Our Lady of Guadalupe, Mystical Rose, make intercession for the Holy Church, protect the Sovereign Pontiff, help all those who invoke thee in their necessities, and since thou art the Blessed Virgin Mary, and Mother of the True God, obtain for us from thy most holy Son the grace of keeping our faith, of sweet hope in the midst of the bitterness of life, of burning charity, and the most precious gift of perseverance so that we may carry our cross cheerfully.

St Josemaría Escrivá and Blessed Alvaro del Portillo visit the Carmelites.

Day Twenty-Six: False Pride.

"As the trustees of certain talents, both supernatural and human, which you must make good use of, draw your own practical conclusions for your daily life. And, at the same time, get rid of the ridiculous delusion that you have something that belongs to you alone as if it were the fruit of your own efforts. Remember there is an ever-present factor, God, which no one can ignore."

-St Josemaría Escrivá

Prayer Intention

Lord Jesus Christ, I humbly beg of You to keep me ever so vigilant so that I do not fall into the temptation of the sins of pride and vanity. Dear Lord, I am a sinner that has offended You with prideful, vain behaviour. I know that through the sacraments, and through humbling myself to You, dear Lord, I can truly love my neighbour and not think of myself as a superior being. Everything that I am capable of, and all that I have is because of You, God. To You and You alone, I owe all glory and I must always strive to see You in others.

"For if anyone thinks he is something, when he is nothing, he deceives himself. But each one must examine his own work, and then he will have reason for boasting in regard to himself alone, and not in regard to another. For each one will bear his own load. The one who is taught The Word is to share all good things with the one who teaches him."

- Galatians 6:3-6

Day Twenty-Six: False Pride.

Dear Lord, I humbly beg You, through the intercession of St Josemaría Escrivá, for the grace to fill my heart and mind with a spirit of thanksgiving, so that I do not take for myself any of the gifts which You have given to me. These gifts may be beauty, wealth, intelligence, or anything else. Everything I have and all that I am is because of You and Your love for me dear Lord. These gifts are for serving You, not for myself.

Prayer to St Josemaría Escrivá

Most loving God, through the mediation of Our Lady, the Blessed Virgin, You chose St Josemaría Escrivá to serve You and honour you. You have gifted St Josemaría Escrivá the wisdom and grace to form Opus Dei, a way of sanctification in daily work and in the fulfilment of the Christian's ordinary life and duties. Grant that I too may learn to turn my everyday life into one that serves You God, and imitates the way of St Josemaría Escrivá with a zeal for loving all souls and striving for sanctification. Grant unto me God, through the intercession of St Josemaría Escrivá the favour of (intention).

Day Twenty-Six: False Pride.

"For all that is in the world—the desires of the flesh and the desires of the eyes and pride in possessions—is not from the Father but is from the world"

\- 1 John 2:16

Holy Rosary of Sorrowful Mysteries

I believe in God, the Father Almighty, Creator of Heaven, and earth; and in Jesus Christ, His only Son, Our Lord, who was conceived by the Holy Ghost, born of the Virgin Mary, suffered under Pontius Pilate, was crucified; died, and was buried. He descended into Hell; the third day He arose again from the dead; He ascended into Heaven, sitteth at the right hand of God, the Father Almighty; from thence He shall come to judge the living and the dead. I believe in the Holy Spirit, the holy Catholic Church, the communion of saints, the forgiveness of sins, the resurrection of the body, and life everlasting.

Our Father, who art in heaven, hallowed be Thy name; Thy kingdom come; Thy will be done on earth as it is in heaven. Give us this day our daily bread; and forgive us our trespasses as we forgive those who trespass against us; and lead us not into temptation, but deliver us from evil.

Hail Mary, full of grace. The Lord is with thee. Blessed art thou among women, and blessed is the fruit of thy womb, Jesus. Holy Mary, Mother of God, pray for us sinners, now and at the hour of our death.

Glory be to the Father, to the Son, and to the Holy Spirit, as it was, is now, and ever shall be, world without end. Amen.

The Five Sorrowful Mysteries are prayed Tuesday and Friday.

The Sorrowful Mysteries remind the faithful of Christ's Passion and His Crucifixion:

The Agony of Jesus in the Garden (Matthew 26:36–56); The Scourging at the Pillar (Matthew 27:26) The Crowning with Thorns (Matthew 27:27–31); The Carrying of the Cross (Matthew 27:32) The Crucifixion (Matthew 27:33–56)

Hail Holy Queen

Hail, Holy Queen, Mother of mercy, our life, our sweetness, and our hope. To thee do we cry, poor banished children of Eve, to thee do we send up our sighs, mourning and weeping in this vale of tears. Turn then, most gracious advocate, thine eyes of mercy toward us; and after this our exile show unto us the blessed fruit of thy womb Jesus, O clement, O loving, O sweet Virgin Mary.

Pray for us, O holy Mother of God. That we may be made worthy of the promises of Christ.

O God, whose only begotten Son, by His life, death, and resurrection, has purchased for us the rewards of eternal salvation; grant we beseech Thee, that meditating upon these mysteries of the most holy Rosary of the Blessed Virgin Mary, we may imitate what they contain and obtain what they promise, through the same Christ our Lord.

Prayer to Our Lady of Guadalupe

Our Lady of Guadalupe, Mystical Rose, make intercession for the Holy Church, protect the Sovereign Pontiff, help all those who invoke thee in their necessities, and since thou art the Blessed Virgin Mary, and Mother of the True God, obtain for us from thy most holy Son the grace of keeping our faith, of sweet hope in the midst of the bitterness of life, of burning charity, and the most precious gift of perseverance so that we may carry our cross cheerfully.

St Josemaría Escrivá with Father Salvador Canals.

Day Twenty-Seven: Discipleship.

"Let us turn to Our Lady, the prudent and faithful Virgin, and to St Joseph, her husband, the perfect model of the just man. They, who lived the virtues we have just contemplated in the presence of Jesus, the Son of God, will obtain for us the grace we need to have the same virtues rooted in our souls, so that we may resolve always to behave as good disciples of the Master: prudent, just and full of charity."

-St Josemaría Escrivá

Prayer Intention

Lord Jesus Christ, I desire to model my life on the virtues of Our lady and St Joseph. I humbly ask of You, to fill me with the spirit of a good disciple so that I may serve You with a heart that is prudent, just and charitable just like Our Lady and St Joseph. Dear Lord, I know that I can grow in these virtues through devotional prayer, spiritual direction, attending Mass and partaking in the sacraments. I know that if I persevere, that I can devote my ordinary life to You, dear Lord, just as Our Lady and St Joseph served You through their ordinary life and devoted themselves to You and Your most Holy Will.

"Little children, I am with you a little while longer. You will seek Me; and as I said to the Jews, now I also say to you, 'Where I am going, you cannot come.' A new commandment I give to you, that you love one another, even as I have loved you, that you also love one another. By this all men will know that you are My disciples, if you have love for one another."

- John 13:33-35

Day Twenty-Seven: Discipleship.

Dear Lord, I humbly beg You, through the intercession of St Josemaría Escrivá, for the grace to transform my heart into one of true discipleship. I desire to live each day following You, sweet Jesus. Please take from me all that I have to offer, so that I may focus on the Mission of the Church and spread Your loving word.

Prayer to St Josemaría Escrivá

Most loving God, through the mediation of Our Lady, the Blessed Virgin, You chose St Josemaría Escrivá to serve You and honour you. You have gifted St Josemaría Escrivá the wisdom and grace to form Opus Dei, a way of sanctification in daily work and in the fulfilment of the Christian's ordinary life and duties. Grant that I too may learn to turn my everyday life into one that serves You God, and imitates the way of St Josemaría Escrivá with a zeal for loving all souls and striving for sanctification. Grant unto me God, through the intercession of St Josemaría Escrivá the favour of (intention).

Day Twenty-Seven: Discipleship.

"Go therefore and make disciples of all nations, baptizing them in the name of the Father and of the Son and of the Holy Spirit, teaching them to observe all that I have commanded you. And behold, I am with you always, to the end of the age."

\- Matthew 28:19-20

Holy Rosary of Glorious Mysteries

I believe in God, the Father Almighty, Creator of Heaven, and earth; and in Jesus Christ, His only Son, Our Lord, who was conceived by the Holy Ghost, born of the Virgin Mary, suffered under Pontius Pilate, was crucified; died, and was buried. He descended into Hell; the third day He arose again from the dead; He ascended into Heaven, sitteth at the right hand of God, the Father Almighty; from thence He shall come to judge the living and the dead. I believe in the Holy Spirit, the holy Catholic Church, the communion of saints, the forgiveness of sins, the resurrection of the body, and life everlasting.

Our Father, who art in heaven, hallowed be Thy name; Thy kingdom come; Thy will be done on earth as it is in heaven. Give us this day our daily bread; and forgive us our trespasses as we forgive those who trespass against us; and lead us not into temptation, but deliver us from evil.

Hail Mary, full of grace. The Lord is with thee. Blessed art thou among women, and blessed is the fruit of thy womb, Jesus. Holy Mary, Mother of God, pray for us sinners, now and at the hour of our death.

Glory be to the Father, to the Son, and to the Holy Spirit, as it was, is now, and ever shall be, world without end. Amen.

The Five Glorious Mysteries are prayed Wednesday and Sunday.

The Glorious Mysteries remind the faithful of Christ's Resurrection and Heaven's glories:

The Resurrection (Luke 24:1-12); The Ascension (Acts 1:6-11) The Descent of the Holy Spirit (Acts 2:1-4); The Assumption (Munificentissimus Deus 44) The Coronation of Mary as Queen of Heaven (Revelations 12:1-6)

Hail Holy Queen

Hail, Holy Queen, Mother of mercy, our life, our sweetness, and our hope. To thee do we cry, poor banished children of Eve, to thee do we send up our sighs, mourning and weeping in this vale of tears. Turn then, most gracious advocate, thine eyes of mercy toward us; and after this our exile show unto us the blessed fruit of thy womb Jesus, O clement, O loving, O sweet Virgin Mary.

Pray for us, O holy Mother of God. That we may be made worthy of the promises of Christ.

O God, whose only begotten Son, by His life, death, and resurrection, has purchased for us the rewards of eternal salvation; grant we beseech Thee, that meditating upon these mysteries of the most holy Rosary of the Blessed Virgin Mary, we may imitate what they contain and obtain what they promise, through the same Christ our Lord.

Prayer to Our Lady of Guadalupe

Our Lady of Guadalupe, Mystical Rose, make intercession for the Holy Church, protect the Sovereign Pontiff, help all those who invoke thee in their necessities, and since thou art the Blessed Virgin Mary, and Mother of the True God, obtain for us from thy most holy Son the grace of keeping our faith, of sweet hope in the midst of the bitterness of life, of burning charity, and the most precious gift of perseverance so that we may carry our cross cheerfully.

St Josemaría Escrivá

Day Twenty-Eight: Vocation.

"Let us ask Our Lord Jesus for light, and beg Him to help us discover, at every moment, the divine meaning which transforms our professional work into the hinge on which our calling to sanctity rests and turns. In the Gospel you will find that Jesus was known as Faber, Filius Mariae, the Workman, Son of Mary. Well, we too, with a holy pride, have to prove with deeds that we are workers, men and women who really work!"

-St Josemaría Escrivá

Prayer Intention

Lord Jesus Christ, I humbly ask of You to gently guide me down the path toward the narrow gate which is wide and leads to destruction. I pray that You light the path which illuminates Your Divinity, and most Holy Will for my vocation as Your follower, dear Lord. Through Your strength with which You carried The Cross to Crucifixion, I can carry out my duties and work hard, embracing each moment with gratitude as I devote my work to You and sanctify my ordinary life.

"Commit your work to the Lord, and your plans will be established. The LORD made everything answerable to him, including the wicked at the time of trouble. The Lord detests those who are proud; truly they will not go unpunished. Iniquity is atoned for by gracious love and truth, and through fear of the Lord, people turn from evil.

- Proverbs 16:3-6

Day Twenty-Eight: Vocation.

Dear Lord, I humbly beg You, through the intercession of St Josemaría Escrivá, for the grace to commit to my vocation in accordance to Your word and most Holy Will. Through studying, hard work, attending the sacraments and prayer, I know that I can devote my work and my life to You, with gratitude and joy.

Prayer to St Josemaría Escrivá

Most loving God, through the mediation of Our Lady, the Blessed Virgin, You chose St Josemaría Escrivá to serve You and honour you. You have gifted St Josemaría Escrivá the wisdom and grace to form Opus Dei, a way of sanctification in daily work and in the fulfilment of the Christian's ordinary life and duties. Grant that I too may learn to turn my everyday life into one that serves You God, and imitates the way of St Josemaría Escrivá with a zeal for loving all souls and striving for sanctification. Grant unto me God, through the intercession of St Josemaría Escrivá the favour of (intention).

Day Twenty-Eight: Vocation.

"Whatever you do, work heartily, as for the Lord and not for men, knowing that from the Lord you will receive the inheritance as your reward. You are serving the Lord Christ. For the wrongdoer will be paid back for the wrong he has done, and there is no partiality."

- Colossians 3:23-25

Holy Rosary of Luminous Mysteries

I believe in God, the Father Almighty, Creator of Heaven, and earth; and in Jesus Christ, His only Son, Our Lord, who was conceived by the Holy Ghost, born of the Virgin Mary, suffered under Pontius Pilate, was crucified; died, and was buried. He descended into Hell; the third day He arose again from the dead; He ascended into Heaven, sitteth at the right hand of God, the Father Almighty; from thence He shall come to judge the living and the dead. I believe in the Holy Spirit, the holy Catholic Church, the communion of saints, the forgiveness of sins, the resurrection of the body, and life everlasting.

Our Father, who art in heaven, hallowed be Thy name; Thy kingdom come; Thy will be done on earth as it is in heaven. Give us this day our daily bread; and forgive us our trespasses as we forgive those who trespass against us; and lead us not into temptation, but deliver us from evil.

Hail Mary, full of grace. The Lord is with thee. Blessed art thou among women, and blessed is the fruit of thy womb, Jesus. Holy Mary, Mother of God, pray for us sinners, now and at the hour of our death.

Glory be to the Father, to the Son, and to the Holy Spirit, as it was, is now, and ever shall be, world without end. Amen.

The Five Luminous Mysteries are prayed on Thursday.

The Luminous Mysteries remind the faithful of Christ's shining light:

The Baptism in the River Jordan (Matthew 3:13–16); The Wedding Feast at Cana (John 2:1–11) The Preaching of the coming of the Kingdom of God (Mark 1:14–15)
The Transfiguration (Matthew 17:1–8); The Institution of the Holy Eucharist (Matthew 26)

Hail Holy Queen

Hail, Holy Queen, Mother of mercy, our life, our sweetness, and our hope. To thee do we cry, poor banished children of Eve, to thee do we send up our sighs, mourning and weeping in this vale of tears. Turn then, most gracious advocate, thine eyes of mercy toward us; and after this our exile show unto us the blessed fruit of thy womb Jesus, O clement, O loving, O sweet Virgin Mary.

Pray for us, O holy Mother of God. That we may be made worthy of the promises of Christ.

O God, whose only begotten Son, by His life, death, and resurrection, has purchased for us the rewards of eternal salvation; grant we beseech Thee, that meditating upon these mysteries of the most holy Rosary of the Blessed Virgin Mary, we may imitate what they contain and obtain what they promise, through the same Christ our Lord.

Prayer to Our Lady of Guadalupe

Our Lady of Guadalupe, Mystical Rose, make intercession for the Holy Church, protect the Sovereign Pontiff, help all those who invoke thee in their necessities, and since thou art the Blessed Virgin Mary, and Mother of the True God, obtain for us from thy most holy Son the grace of keeping our faith, of sweet hope in the midst of the bitterness of life, of burning charity, and the most precious gift of perseverance so that we may carry our cross cheerfully.

St Josemaría Escrivá celebrates the Holy Mass.

Day Twenty-Nine: Ecumenism.

"It would be a false charity, a diabolical, deceitful charity, to give way in matters of faith. We must be fortes in fide — strong in faith, firm, as Saint Peter demands. This is not fanaticism, but quite simply the practice of our faith. It does not entail disliking anyone. We can give way in all accidental matters, but in matters of faith we cannot give way. We cannot spare the oil from our lamps, otherwise when the Bridegroom comes he will find they have burned out."

-St Josemaría Escrivá

Prayer Intention

Lord Jesus Christ, I desire to understand those who adhere to a different belief and to recognise them as Your children. I humbly ask of You to fill my heart with Your most loving compassion so that I may help to lead all souls closer to You, through witness of Your most Sacred Heart which loves every human on earth. Lord Jesus Christ, You are the Truth of which all of humanity seeks. I desire to show the world what it means to be loved by You and to love You. Please give me the ability to see You in all who are created in Your image, so that they may be shown the love of which You command of us toward one another.

"For all of you who were baptized into Christ have clothed yourselves with Christ. There is neither Jew nor Greek, there is neither slave nor free, there is no male and female, for you are all one in Christ Jesus."

- Galatians 3:27-28

Day Twenty-Nine: Ecumenism.

Dear Lord, I humbly beg You, through the intercession of St Josemaría Escrivá, for the grace to commit to myself to being patient, compassionate, and understanding toward those who are not of the Christian faith, so that I may lead them closer to You and be a witness to Your infinite love and mercy.

Prayer to St Josemaría Escrivá

Most loving God, through the mediation of Our Lady, the Blessed Virgin, You chose St Josemaría Escrivá to serve You and honour you. You have gifted St Josemaría Escrivá the wisdom and grace to form Opus Dei, a way of sanctification in daily work and in the fulfilment of the Christian's ordinary life and duties. Grant that I too may learn to turn my everyday life into one that serves You God, and imitates the way of St Josemaría Escrivá with a zeal for loving all souls and striving for sanctification. Grant unto me God, through the intercession of St Josemaría Escrivá the favour of (intention).

Day Twenty-Nine: Ecumenism.

"In the same way, let your light shine before others, so that they may see your good works and give glory to your Father who is in heaven"

- Matthew 5:16

Holy Rosary of Joyful Mysteries

I believe in God, the Father Almighty, Creator of Heaven, and earth; and in Jesus Christ, His only Son, Our Lord, who was conceived by the Holy Ghost, born of the Virgin Mary, suffered under Pontius Pilate, was crucified; died, and was buried. He descended into Hell; the third day He arose again from the dead; He ascended into Heaven, sitteth at the right hand of God, the Father Almighty; from thence He shall come to judge the living and the dead. I believe in the Holy Spirit, the holy Catholic Church, the communion of saints, the forgiveness of sins, the resurrection of the body, and life everlasting.

Our Father, who art in heaven, hallowed be Thy name; Thy kingdom come; Thy will be done on earth as it is in heaven. Give us this day our daily bread; and forgive us our trespasses as we forgive those who trespass against us; and lead us not into temptation, but deliver us from evil.

Hail Mary, full of grace. The Lord is with thee. Blessed art thou among women, and blessed is the fruit of thy womb, Jesus. Holy Mary, Mother of God, pray for us sinners, now and at the hour of our death.

Glory be to the Father, to the Son, and to the Holy Spirit, as it was, is now, and ever shall be, world without end. Amen.

The Five Joyful Mysteries are prayed Monday and Saturday.

The Joyful Mysteries remind the faithful of Our Lady's Fiat and Christ's birth:

The Annunciation (Luke 1:26–38); The Visitation (Luke 1:39–56) The Nativity (Luke 2:1–21); The Presentation (Luke 2:22–38) The Finding of the Child Jesus in the Temple (Luke 2:41–52)

Hail Holy Queen

Hail, Holy Queen, Mother of mercy, our life, our sweetness, and our hope. To thee do we cry, poor banished children of Eve, to thee do we send up our sighs, mourning and weeping in this vale of tears. Turn then, most gracious advocate, thine eyes of mercy toward us; and after this our exile show unto us the blessed fruit of thy womb Jesus, O clement, O loving, O sweet Virgin Mary.

Pray for us, O holy Mother of God. That we may be made worthy of the promises of Christ.

O God, whose only begotten Son, by His life, death, and resurrection, has purchased for us the rewards of eternal salvation; grant we beseech Thee, that meditating upon these mysteries of the most holy Rosary of the Blessed Virgin Mary, we may imitate what they contain and obtain what they promise, through the same Christ our Lord.

Prayer to Our Lady of Guadalupe

Our Lady of Guadalupe, Mystical Rose, make intercession for the Holy Church, protect the Sovereign Pontiff, help all those who invoke thee in their necessities, and since thou art the Blessed Virgin Mary, and Mother of the True God, obtain for us from thy most holy Son the grace of keeping our faith, of sweet hope in the midst of the bitterness of life, of burning charity, and the most precious gift of perseverance so that we may carry our cross cheerfully.

St Josemaría Escrivá and Blessed Alvaro del Portillo at the University of Navarra in 1960.

Day Thirty: The Magisterium.

"There is no other possible attitude for a Catholic: we have to defend the authority of the Pope always, and to be ready always to correct our own views with docility, in line with the teaching authority of the Church. In so far as you can, you should fight against the conspiracy of silence they want to muzzle the Church with. Some people stop her voice being heard; others will not let the good example of those who preach with their deeds be seen; others wipe out every trace of good doctrine...and so very many cannot bear to hear her. Don't be scared, I say again. But don't get tired, either, of your task of being a loudspeaker for the teachings of the Magisterium."

-St Josemaría Escrivá

Prayer Intention

Lord Jesus Christ, I humbly ask of you to give me the strength and humility to fully submit to the Magisterium of the Church, which You have founded. I know that at times I may struggle in my docility and obedience, and it is during these times dear Lord, that I ask you to illuminate the darkness and lead me down the path of righteousness, in accordance with the teachings and traditions of the Church.

"Now I commend you because you remember me in everything and maintain the traditions even as I delivered them to you."

- 1 Corinthians 11:2

Day Thirty: The Magisterium.

Dear Lord, I humbly beg You, through the intercession of St Josemaría Escrivá, for the grace to always defend the Holy Father, and to defend the Magisterium of the Catholic Church, living in accordance to her teachings. I know that I can attain this through prayer, the sacraments and reading the Catechism.

Prayer to St Josemaría Escrivá

Most loving God, through the mediation of Our Lady, the Blessed Virgin, You chose St Josemaría Escrivá to serve You and honour you. You have gifted St Josemaría Escrivá the wisdom and grace to form Opus Dei, a way of sanctification in daily work and in the fulfilment of the Christian's ordinary life and duties. Grant that I too may learn to turn my everyday life into one that serves You God, and imitates the way of St Josemaría Escrivá with a zeal for loving all souls and striving for sanctification. Grant unto me God, through the intercession of St Josemaría Escrivá the favour of (intention).

Day Thirty: The Magisterium.

"See to it that no one takes you captive by philosophy and empty deceit, according to human tradition, according to the elemental spirits of the world, and not according to Christ."

- Colossians 2:8

Holy Rosary of Sorrowful Mysteries

I believe in God, the Father Almighty, Creator of Heaven, and earth; and in Jesus Christ, His only Son, Our Lord, who was conceived by the Holy Ghost, born of the Virgin Mary, suffered under Pontius Pilate, was crucified; died, and was buried. He descended into Hell; the third day He arose again from the dead; He ascended into Heaven, sitteth at the right hand of God, the Father Almighty; from thence He shall come to judge the living and the dead. I believe in the Holy Spirit, the holy Catholic Church, the communion of saints, the forgiveness of sins, the resurrection of the body, and life everlasting.

Our Father, who art in heaven, hallowed be Thy name; Thy kingdom come; Thy will be done on earth as it is in heaven. Give us this day our daily bread; and forgive us our trespasses as we forgive those who trespass against us; and lead us not into temptation, but deliver us from evil.

Hail Mary, full of grace. The Lord is with thee. Blessed art thou among women, and blessed is the fruit of thy womb, Jesus. Holy Mary, Mother of God, pray for us sinners, now and at the hour of our death.

Glory be to the Father, to the Son, and to the Holy Spirit, as it was, is now, and ever shall be, world without end. Amen.

The Five Sorrowful Mysteries are prayed Tuesday and Friday.

The Sorrowful Mysteries remind the faithful of Christ's Passion and of His Crucifixion:

The Agony of Jesus in the Garden (Matthew 26:36–56); The Scourging at the Pillar (Matthew 27:26) The Crowning with Thorns (Matthew 27:27–31); The Carrying of the Cross (Matthew 27:32) The Crucifixion (Matthew 27:33–56)

Hail Holy Queen

Hail, Holy Queen, Mother of mercy, our life, our sweetness, and our hope. To thee do we cry, poor banished children of Eve, to thee do we send up our sighs, mourning and weeping in this vale of tears. Turn then, most gracious advocate, thine eyes of mercy toward us; and after this our exile show unto us the blessed fruit of thy womb Jesus, O clement, O loving, O sweet Virgin Mary.

Pray for us, O holy Mother of God. That we may be made worthy of the promises of Christ.

O God, whose only begotten Son, by His life, death, and resurrection, has purchased for us the rewards of eternal salvation; grant we beseech Thee, that meditating upon these mysteries of the most holy Rosary of the Blessed Virgin Mary, we may imitate what they contain and obtain what they promise, through the same Christ our Lord.

Prayer to Our Lady of Guadalupe

Our Lady of Guadalupe, Mystical Rose, make intercession for the Holy Church, protect the Sovereign Pontiff, help all those who invoke thee in their necessities, and since thou art the Blessed Virgin Mary, and Mother of the True God, obtain for us from thy most holy Son the grace of keeping our faith, of sweet hope in the midst of the bitterness of life, of burning charity, and the most precious gift of perseverance so that we may carry our cross cheerfully.

St Josemaría Escrivá venerates the Tilma of Our Lady of Guadalupe.

Day Thirty-One: The Holy Eucharist.

"When you receive Our Lord in the Holy Eucharist, thank Him from the bottom of your heart for being so good as to be with you. Have you ever stopped to consider that it took centuries and centuries before the Messiah came? All those patriarchs and prophets praying together with the whole people of Israel: Come, Lord, the land is parched! If only your loving expectation were like this."

-St Josemaría Escrivá

Prayer Intention

Lord Jesus Christ, I humbly ask of you to fill my heart with reverence for Your most Holy Presence in the Eucharist, which is the Blessed Sacrament. I pray that You renew my heart each and every day, with gratitude that I am privileged to adore You at the Tabernacle. Dear Lord, You are the Divine Master who was crucified for the redemption of sinners. Through my sins, I have crucified You as well. Yet because You are ever merciful and Your Sacred Heart overflows with love eternal, You have risen to sustain me.

"I am the bread of life. Your fathers ate the manna in the wilderness, and they died. This is the bread which comes down out of heaven, so that one may eat of it and not die. I am the living bread that came down from heaven. If anyone eats of this bread, he will live forever. And the bread that I will give for the life of the world is my flesh."

- John 6:48-51

Day Thirty-One: The Holy Eucharist.

Dear Lord, I humbly beg You, through the intercession of St Josemaría Escrivá, for the grace to stand or kneel before You in the Holy Eucharist with a heart full of humility and reverence, in communion with You. You have seen the worth in humanity, and for You it was worth your life, dear Lord Jesus. Without this most Blessed Sacrament, and Your sacrifice, there would be no salvation for mankind.

Prayer to St Josemaría Escrivá

Most loving God, through the mediation of Our Lady, the Blessed Virgin, You chose St Josemaría Escrivá to serve You and honour you. You have gifted St Josemaría Escrivá the wisdom and grace to form Opus Dei, a way of sanctification in daily work and in the fulfilment of the Christian's ordinary life and duties. Grant that I too may learn to turn my everyday life into one that serves You God, and imitates the way of St Josemaría Escrivá with a zeal for loving all souls and striving for sanctification. Grant unto me God, through the intercession of St Josemaría Escrivá the favour of (intention).

Day Thirty-One: The Holy Eucharist.

"For as often as you eat this bread and drink the cup, you proclaim the Lord's death until He comes."

- 1 Corinthians 11:26

Holy Rosary of Glorious Mysteries

I believe in God, the Father Almighty, Creator of Heaven, and earth; and in Jesus Christ, His only Son, Our Lord, who was conceived by the Holy Ghost, born of the Virgin Mary, suffered under Pontius Pilate, was crucified; died, and was buried. He descended into Hell; the third day He arose again from the dead; He ascended into Heaven, sitteth at the right hand of God, the Father Almighty; from thence He shall come to judge the living and the dead. I believe in the Holy Spirit, the holy Catholic Church, the communion of saints, the forgiveness of sins, the resurrection of the body, and life everlasting.

Our Father, who art in heaven, hallowed be Thy name; Thy kingdom come; Thy will be done on earth as it is in heaven. Give us this day our daily bread; and forgive us our trespasses as we forgive those who trespass against us; and lead us not into temptation, but deliver us from evil.

Hail Mary, full of grace. The Lord is with thee. Blessed art thou among women, and blessed is the fruit of thy womb, Jesus. Holy Mary, Mother of God, pray for us sinners, now and at the hour of our death.

Glory be to the Father, to the Son, and to the Holy Spirit, as it was, is now, and ever shall be, world without end. Amen.

The Five Glorious Mysteries are prayed Wednesday and Sunday.

The Glorious Mysteries remind the faithful of Christ's Resurrection and Heaven's glories:

The Resurrection (Luke 24:1-12); The Ascension (Acts 1:6-11) The Descent of the Holy Spirit (Acts 2:1-4); The Assumption (Munificentissimus Deus 44) The Coronation of Mary as Queen of Heaven (Revelations 12:1-6)

Hail Holy Queen

Hail, Holy Queen, Mother of mercy, our life, our sweetness, and our hope. To thee do we cry, poor banished children of Eve, to thee do we send up our sighs, mourning and weeping in this vale of tears. Turn then, most gracious advocate, thine eyes of mercy toward us; and after this our exile show unto us the blessed fruit of thy womb Jesus, O clement, O loving, O sweet Virgin Mary.

Pray for us, O holy Mother of God. That we may be made worthy of the promises of Christ.

O God, whose only begotten Son, by His life, death, and resurrection, has purchased for us the rewards of eternal salvation; grant we beseech Thee, that meditating upon these mysteries of the most holy Rosary of the Blessed Virgin Mary, we may imitate what they contain and obtain what they promise, through the same Christ our Lord.

Prayer to Our Lady of Guadalupe

Our Lady of Guadalupe, Mystical Rose, make intercession for the Holy Church, protect the Sovereign Pontiff, help all those who invoke thee in their necessities, and since thou art the Blessed Virgin Mary, and Mother of the True God, obtain for us from thy most holy Son the grace of keeping our faith, of sweet hope in the midst of the bitterness of life, of burning charity, and the most precious gift of perseverance so that we may carry our cross cheerfully.

St Josemaría Escrivá administers the Blessed Sacrament to the faithful.

Day Thirty-Two: Confession.

"If ever you fall, go quickly to Confession and seek spiritual guidance. Show your wound, so that it gets properly healed and all possibility of infection is removed, even if doing this hurts you as much as having an operation. In the sacrament of Penance, Jesus forgives us. Christ's merits are applied to us there. It is for love of us that He is on the Cross with his arms stretched out, fastened to the wood more by the Love He has for us than by the nails."

-St Josemaría Escrivá

Prayer Intention

Lord Jesus Christ, I humbly ask of you to give me the strength to humble myself and open my heart to fully trusting in You and Your remissio aeterna, the eternal forgiveness which You have so generously provided to me, a sinner, through the sacrament of confession. You await me with open arms, because You are Most Precious and ever loving. I pray that I will always come to you, ready to persevere on the path toward sainthood as I walk the Way of The Cross with You, Dear Lord.

"But when the kindness of God our Saviour and His love for mankind appeared, He saved us, not because of works done by us in righteousness, but according to His own mercy, by the washing of regeneration and renewal of the Holy Spirit He poured out this Spirit on us abundantly through Jesus Christ our Saviour."

- Titus 3:4-6

Day Thirty-Two: Confession.

Dear Lord, I humbly beg You, through the intercession of St Josemaría Escrivá, for the grace to approach You in the sacrament of confession, seeking forgiveness with the contrite heart of a sinner in need of Your endless mercy and love. I pray that I will never lose hope, that I may always seek absolution so that my soul may be rectified, that I come to see the error of my ways and with Your grace, lead a holier life.

Prayer to St Josemaría Escrivá

Most loving God, through the mediation of Our Lady, the Blessed Virgin, You chose St Josemaría Escrivá to serve You and honour you. You have gifted St Josemaría Escrivá the wisdom and grace to form Opus Dei, a way of sanctification in daily work and in the fulfilment of the Christian's ordinary life and duties. Grant that I too may learn to turn my everyday life into one that serves You God, and imitates the way of St Josemaría Escrivá with a zeal for loving all souls and striving for sanctification. Grant unto me God, through the intercession of St Josemaría Escrivá the favour of (intention).

Day Thirty-Two: Confession.

"If we confess our sins, He is faithful and just to forgive us our sins and to cleanse us from all unrighteousness."

\- 1 John 1:9

Holy Rosary of Luminous Mysteries

I believe in God, the Father Almighty, Creator of Heaven, and earth; and in Jesus Christ, His only Son, Our Lord, who was conceived by the Holy Ghost, born of the Virgin Mary, suffered under Pontius Pilate, was crucified; died, and was buried. He descended into Hell; the third day He arose again from the dead; He ascended into Heaven, sitteth at the right hand of God, the Father Almighty; from thence He shall come to judge the living and the dead. I believe in the Holy Spirit, the holy Catholic Church, the communion of saints, the forgiveness of sins, the resurrection of the body, and life everlasting.

Our Father, who art in heaven, hallowed be Thy name; Thy kingdom come; Thy will be done on earth as it is in heaven. Give us this day our daily bread; and forgive us our trespasses as we forgive those who trespass against us; and lead us not into temptation, but deliver us from evil.

Hail Mary, full of grace. The Lord is with thee. Blessed art thou among women, and blessed is the fruit of thy womb, Jesus. Holy Mary, Mother of God, pray for us sinners, now and at the hour of our death.

Glory be to the Father, to the Son, and to the Holy Spirit, as it was, is now, and ever shall be, world without end. Amen.

The Five Luminous Mysteries are prayed on Thursday.

The Luminous Mysteries remind the faithful of Christ's shining light:

The Baptism in the River Jordan (Matthew 3:13–16); The Wedding Feast at Cana (John 2:1–11) The Preaching of the coming of the Kingdom of God (Mark 1:14–15) The Transfiguration (Matthew 17:1–8); The Institution of the Holy Eucharist (Matthew 26)

Hail Holy Queen

Hail, Holy Queen, Mother of mercy, our life, our sweetness, and our hope. To thee do we cry, poor banished children of Eve, to thee do we send up our sighs, mourning and weeping in this vale of tears. Turn then, most gracious advocate, thine eyes of mercy toward us; and after this our exile show unto us the blessed fruit of thy womb Jesus, O clement, O loving, O sweet Virgin Mary.

Pray for us, O holy Mother of God. That we may be made worthy of the promises of Christ.

O God, whose only begotten Son, by His life, death, and resurrection, has purchased for us the rewards of eternal salvation; grant we beseech Thee, that meditating upon these mysteries of the most holy Rosary of the Blessed Virgin Mary, we may imitate what they contain and obtain what they promise, through the same Christ our Lord.

.

Prayer to Our Lady of Guadalupe

Our Lady of Guadalupe, Mystical Rose, make intercession for the Holy Church, protect the Sovereign Pontiff, help all those who invoke thee in their necessities, and since thou art the Blessed Virgin Mary, and Mother of the True God, obtain for us from thy most holy Son the grace of keeping our faith, of sweet hope in the midst of the bitterness of life, of burning charity, and the most precious gift of perseverance so that we may carry our cross cheerfully.

St Josemaría Escrivá on the feast of Our Lady's Assumption 1971.

Day Thirty-Three: Divine Worship.

"Love Our Lord very much. Maintain and foster in your soul a sense of urgency to love Him better. Love God precisely now when perhaps a good many of those who hold Him in their hands do not love Him, but rather ill-treat and neglect Him. Be sure to take good care of the Lord for me, in the Holy Mass and throughout the whole day!"

-St Josemaría Escrivá

Prayer Intention

Lord Jesus Christ, I humbly ask of you to fill my heart with love and reverence, so that I may grow each day, closer to You, dear Lord, so that with each sun rise, and starry night sky, I think of You and of all of the many ways in which I can worship You in loving fidelity. In welcoming the stranger, in loving my neighbour, in attending Mass, in prayer and participation in the sacraments, and in loving Your most beautiful and holy mother, the Blessed Virgin.

"But the hour is coming, and is now here, when the true worshipers will worship the Father in spirit and truth, for the Father is seeking such people to worship Him. God is a Spirit: and they that worship him must worship him in spirit and in truth. The woman told him, 'I know that the Anointed One is coming, who is being called the Messiah. When that person comes, he will explain everything.' 'I am he,' Jesus replied, "the one who is speaking to you.'"

- John 4:23

Day Thirty-Three: Divine Worship.

Dear Lord, I humbly beg You, through the intercession of St Josemaría Escrivá, for the grace to love You with all of my heart, as You love me; for I am a sinner but a child in Your fatherly eyes. I pray for the grace to grow more in love each day with You and Your most holy Catholic church. It is only with Your grace and a heart filled with true love for all that is pleasing to You, that I can obtain everlasting life in Heaven.

Prayer to St Josemaría Escrivá

Most loving God, through the mediation of Our Lady, the Blessed Virgin, You chose St Josemaría Escrivá to serve You and honour you. You have gifted St Josemaría Escrivá the wisdom and grace to form Opus Dei, a way of sanctification in daily work and in the fulfilment of the Christian's ordinary life and duties. Grant that I too may learn to turn my everyday life into one that serves You God, and imitates the way of St Josemaría Escrivá with a zeal for loving all souls and striving for sanctification. Grant unto me God, through the intercession of St Josemaría Escrivá the favour of (intention).

Day Thirty-Three: Divine Worship.

"All the nations you have made will come and worship before you, Lord; they will bring glory to your name. For you are great and do marvellous deeds; you alone are God."

- Psalm 86:9-10

Holy Rosary of Joyful Mysteries

I believe in God, the Father Almighty, Creator of Heaven, and earth; and in Jesus Christ, His only Son, Our Lord, who was conceived by the Holy Ghost, born of the Virgin Mary, suffered under Pontius Pilate, was crucified; died, and was buried. He descended into Hell; the third day He arose again from the dead; He ascended into Heaven, sitteth at the right hand of God, the Father Almighty; from thence He shall come to judge the living and the dead. I believe in the Holy Spirit, the holy Catholic Church, the communion of saints, the forgiveness of sins, the resurrection of the body, and life everlasting.

Our Father, who art in heaven, hallowed be Thy name; Thy kingdom come; Thy will be done on earth as it is in heaven. Give us this day our daily bread; and forgive us our trespasses as we forgive those who trespass against us; and lead us not into temptation, but deliver us from evil.

Hail Mary, full of grace. The Lord is with thee. Blessed art thou among women, and blessed is the fruit of thy womb, Jesus. Holy Mary, Mother of God, pray for us sinners, now and at the hour of our death.

Glory be to the Father, to the Son, and to the Holy Spirit, as it was, is now, and ever shall be, world without end. Amen.

The Five Joyful Mysteries are prayed Monday and Saturday.

The Joyful Mysteries remind the faithful of Our Lady's Fiat and Christ's birth:

The Annunciation (Luke 1:26–38); The Visitation (Luke 1:39–56) The Nativity (Luke 2:1–21); The Presentation (Luke 2:22–38) The Finding of the Child Jesus in the Temple (Luke 2:41–52)

Hail Holy Queen

Hail, Holy Queen, Mother of mercy, our life, our sweetness, and our hope. To thee do we cry, poor banished children of Eve, to thee do we send up our sighs, mourning and weeping in this vale of tears. Turn then, most gracious advocate, thine eyes of mercy toward us; and after this our exile show unto us the blessed fruit of thy womb Jesus, O clement, O loving, O sweet Virgin Mary.

Pray for us, O holy Mother of God. That we may be made worthy of the promises of Christ.

O God, whose only begotten Son, by His life, death, and resurrection, has purchased for us the rewards of eternal salvation; grant we beseech Thee, that meditating upon these mysteries of the most holy Rosary of the Blessed Virgin Mary, we may imitate what they contain and obtain what they promise, through the same Christ our Lord.

Prayer to Our Lady of Guadalupe

Our Lady of Guadalupe, Mystical Rose, make intercession for the Holy Church, protect the Sovereign Pontiff, help all those who invoke thee in their necessities, and since thou art the Blessed Virgin Mary, and Mother of the True God, obtain for us from thy most holy Son the grace of keeping our faith, of sweet hope in the midst of the bitterness of life, of burning charity, and the most precious gift of perseverance so that we may carry our cross cheerfully.

St Josemaría Escrivá as Chancellor of the University of Navarra.

Day Thirty-Four: Divine Filiation.

"We are children of God. Bearers of the only flame that can light up the paths of the earth for souls, of the only brightness which can never be darkened, dimmed or overshadowed. The Lord uses us as torches, to make that light shine out...It depends on us that many should not remain in darkness, but walk instead along paths that lead to eternal life."

-St Josemaría Escrivá

Prayer Intention

Lord Jesus Christ, I humbly ask that You set me ablaze with a flaming heart full of love for You, and fill my spirit with zeal for the faith, so that with Your grace and fatherly guidance, I can find the courage to radiate the holy light which You have sparked deep within my soul. It is only with Your grace that the light can shine bright, like endless stars in the night sky. My love for You must be more than mediocre, dear Jesus. My love for You must be dazzling and blinding to satan, so that he cannot prevail in his wicked plan to lead me away from You, my heavenly Father, into discord, or disobedience.

"See what kind of love the Father has given to us, that we should be called children of God; and so we are. The reason why the world does not know us is that it did not know Him."

- 1 John 3:1

Day Thirty-Four: Divine Filiation.

Dear Lord, I humbly beg You, through the intercession of St Josemaría Escrivá, for the humility and love of a child, so that I may look upon you as my Father and know that you have created me as I am, so that I may devote my whole being to loving You, most gracious and ever merciful Christ.

Prayer to St Josemaría Escrivá

Most loving God, through the mediation of Our Lady, the Blessed Virgin, You chose St Josemaría Escrivá to serve You and honour you. You have gifted St Josemaría Escrivá the wisdom and grace to form Opus Dei, a way of sanctification in daily work and in the fulfilment of the Christian's ordinary life and duties. Grant that I too may learn to turn my everyday life into one that serves You God, and imitates the way of St Josemaría Escrivá with a zeal for loving all souls and striving for sanctification. Grant unto me God, through the intercession of St Josemaría Escrivá the favour of (intention).

Day Thirty-Four: Divine Filiation.

"Anyone who does not love, does not know God, because God is love."

- 1 John 4:8

Holy Rosary of Sorrowful Mysteries

I believe in God, the Father Almighty, Creator of Heaven, and earth; and in Jesus Christ, His only Son, Our Lord, who was conceived by the Holy Ghost, born of the Virgin Mary, suffered under Pontius Pilate, was crucified; died, and was buried. He descended into Hell; the third day He arose again from the dead; He ascended into Heaven, sitteth at the right hand of God, the Father Almighty; from thence He shall come to judge the living and the dead. I believe in the Holy Spirit, the holy Catholic Church, the communion of saints, the forgiveness of sins, the resurrection of the body, and life everlasting.

Our Father, who art in heaven, hallowed be Thy name; Thy kingdom come; Thy will be done on earth as it is in heaven. Give us this day our daily bread; and forgive us our trespasses as we forgive those who trespass against us; and lead us not into temptation, but deliver us from evil.

Hail Mary, full of grace. The Lord is with thee. Blessed art thou among women, and blessed is the fruit of thy womb, Jesus. Holy Mary, Mother of God, pray for us sinners, now and at the hour of our death.

Glory be to the Father, to the Son, and to the Holy Spirit, as it was, is now, and ever shall be, world without end. Amen.

The Five Sorrowful Mysteries are prayed Tuesday and Friday.

The Sorrowful Mysteries remind the faithful of Christ's Passion and of His Crucifixion:

The Agony of Jesus in the Garden (Matthew 26:36–56); The Scourging at the Pillar (Matthew 27:26) The Crowning with Thorns (Matthew 27:27–31); The Carrying of the Cross (Matthew 27:32) The Crucifixion (Matthew 27:33–56)

Hail Holy Queen

Hail, Holy Queen, Mother of mercy, our life, our sweetness, and our hope. To thee do we cry, poor banished children of Eve, to thee do we send up our sighs, mourning and weeping in this vale of tears. Turn then, most gracious advocate, thine eyes of mercy toward us; and after this our exile show unto us the blessed fruit of thy womb Jesus, O clement, O loving, O sweet Virgin Mary.

Pray for us, O holy Mother of God. That we may be made worthy of the promises of Christ.

O God, whose only begotten Son, by His life, death, and resurrection, has purchased for us the rewards of eternal salvation; grant we beseech Thee, that meditating upon these mysteries of the most holy Rosary of the Blessed Virgin Mary, we may imitate what they contain and obtain what they promise, through the same Christ our Lord.

Prayer to Our Lady of Guadalupe

Our Lady of Guadalupe, Mystical Rose, make intercession for the Holy Church, protect the Sovereign Pontiff, help all those who invoke thee in their necessities, and since thou art the Blessed Virgin Mary, and Mother of the True God, obtain for us from thy most holy Son the grace of keeping our faith, of sweet hope in the midst of the bitterness of life, of burning charity, and the most precious gift of perseverance so that we may carry our cross cheerfully.

St Josemaría Escrivá and members of Opus Dei at Fatima in 1972.

Day Thirty-Five: Priesthood.

"Since you call yourself a Christian, you have to live the Sacred Liturgy of the Church, putting genuine care into your prayer and mortification for priests, especially for new priests, on the days marked out for this intention, and when you know that they are to receive the Sacrament of Order."

-St Josemaría Escrivá

Prayer Intention

Lord Jesus Christ, I humbly ask that You fill my heart and spirit with love for all of the holy priests which serve You and make their life a never-ending apostolate with a zeal for saving souls. Dear Lord, please help me to grow in obedience, respect, love and admiration for the priesthood, so that I may remember to always pray for priests, to offer up my sufferings, so that You may bless their ministry through mortification and graces so that they may fulfil their vocations, bearing the best of fruits.

"Then I saw thrones, and those who sat on them were given authority to judge. I also saw the souls of those who had been beheaded because of their testimony about Jesus and because of the word of God. They had not worshipped the beast or its image and had not received its mark on their foreheads or hands. They came back to life and ruled with the Messiah for a thousand years. The rest of the dead did not come back to life until the thousand years were over. This is the first resurrection. Holy is the one who shares in the first resurrection! Over such the second death has no power, but they will be priests of God and of Christ, and they will reign with him for a thousand years."

- Revelation 20:4-6

Day Thirty-Five: Priesthood.

Dear Lord, I humbly beg You, through the intercession of St Josemaría Escrivá, for the grace to love the priesthood, and the many priests of your holy church, for they are a living testament to Your sacrifice. I ask that You protect all priests from the wicked snares of the accuser and give me the courage to defend the priesthood against those who would seek to destroy and divide the apostles whom You have appointed.

Prayer to St Josemaría Escrivá

Most loving God, through the mediation of Our Lady, the Blessed Virgin, You chose St Josemaría Escrivá to serve You and honour you. You have gifted St Josemaría Escrivá the wisdom and grace to form Opus Dei, a way of sanctification in daily work and in the fulfilment of the Christian's ordinary life and duties. Grant that I too may learn to turn my everyday life into one that serves You God, and imitates the way of St Josemaría Escrivá with a zeal for loving all souls and striving for sanctification. Grant unto me God, through the intercession of St Josemaría Escrivá the favour of (intention).

Day Thirty-Five: Priesthood.

"For the lips of a priest should guard knowledge, and people should seek instruction from his mouth, for he is the messenger of the Lord of hosts."

\- Malachai 2:7

Holy Rosary of Glorious Mysteries

I believe in God, the Father Almighty, Creator of Heaven, and earth; and in Jesus Christ, His only Son, Our Lord, who was conceived by the Holy Ghost, born of the Virgin Mary, suffered under Pontius Pilate, was crucified; died, and was buried. He descended into Hell; the third day He arose again from the dead; He ascended into Heaven, sitteth at the right hand of God, the Father Almighty; from thence He shall come to judge the living and the dead. I believe in the Holy Spirit, the holy Catholic Church, the communion of saints, the forgiveness of sins, the resurrection of the body, and life everlasting.

Our Father, who art in heaven, hallowed be Thy name; Thy kingdom come; Thy will be done on earth as it is in heaven. Give us this day our daily bread; and forgive us our trespasses as we forgive those who trespass against us; and lead us not into temptation, but deliver us from evil.

Hail Mary, full of grace. The Lord is with thee. Blessed art thou among women, and blessed is the fruit of thy womb, Jesus. Holy Mary, Mother of God, pray for us sinners, now and at the hour of our death.

Glory be to the Father, to the Son, and to the Holy Spirit, as it was, is now, and ever shall be, world without end. Amen.

The Five Glorious Mysteries are prayed Wednesday and Sunday.

The Glorious Mysteries remind the faithful of Christ's Resurrection and Heaven's glories:

The Resurrection (Luke 24:1-12); The Ascension (Acts 1:6-11) The Descent of the Holy Spirit (Acts 2:1-4); The Assumption (Munificentissimus Deus 44) The Coronation of Mary as Queen of Heaven (Revelations 12:1-6)

Hail Holy Queen

Hail, Holy Queen, Mother of mercy, our life, our sweetness, and our hope. To thee do we cry, poor banished children of Eve, to thee do we send up our sighs, mourning and weeping in this vale of tears. Turn then, most gracious advocate, thine eyes of mercy toward us; and after this our exile show unto us the blessed fruit of thy womb Jesus, O clement, O loving, O sweet Virgin Mary.

Pray for us, O holy Mother of God. That we may be made worthy of the promises of Christ.

O God, whose only begotten Son, by His life, death, and resurrection, has purchased for us the rewards of eternal salvation; grant we beseech Thee, that meditating upon these mysteries of the most holy Rosary of the Blessed Virgin Mary, we may imitate what they contain and obtain what they promise, through the same Christ our Lord.

Prayer to Our Lady of Guadalupe

Our Lady of Guadalupe, Mystical Rose, make intercession for the Holy Church, protect the Sovereign Pontiff, help all those who invoke thee in their necessities, and since thou art the Blessed Virgin Mary, and Mother of the True God, obtain for us from thy most holy Son the grace of keeping our faith, of sweet hope in the midst of the bitterness of life, of burning charity, and the most precious gift of perseverance so that we may carry our cross cheerfully.

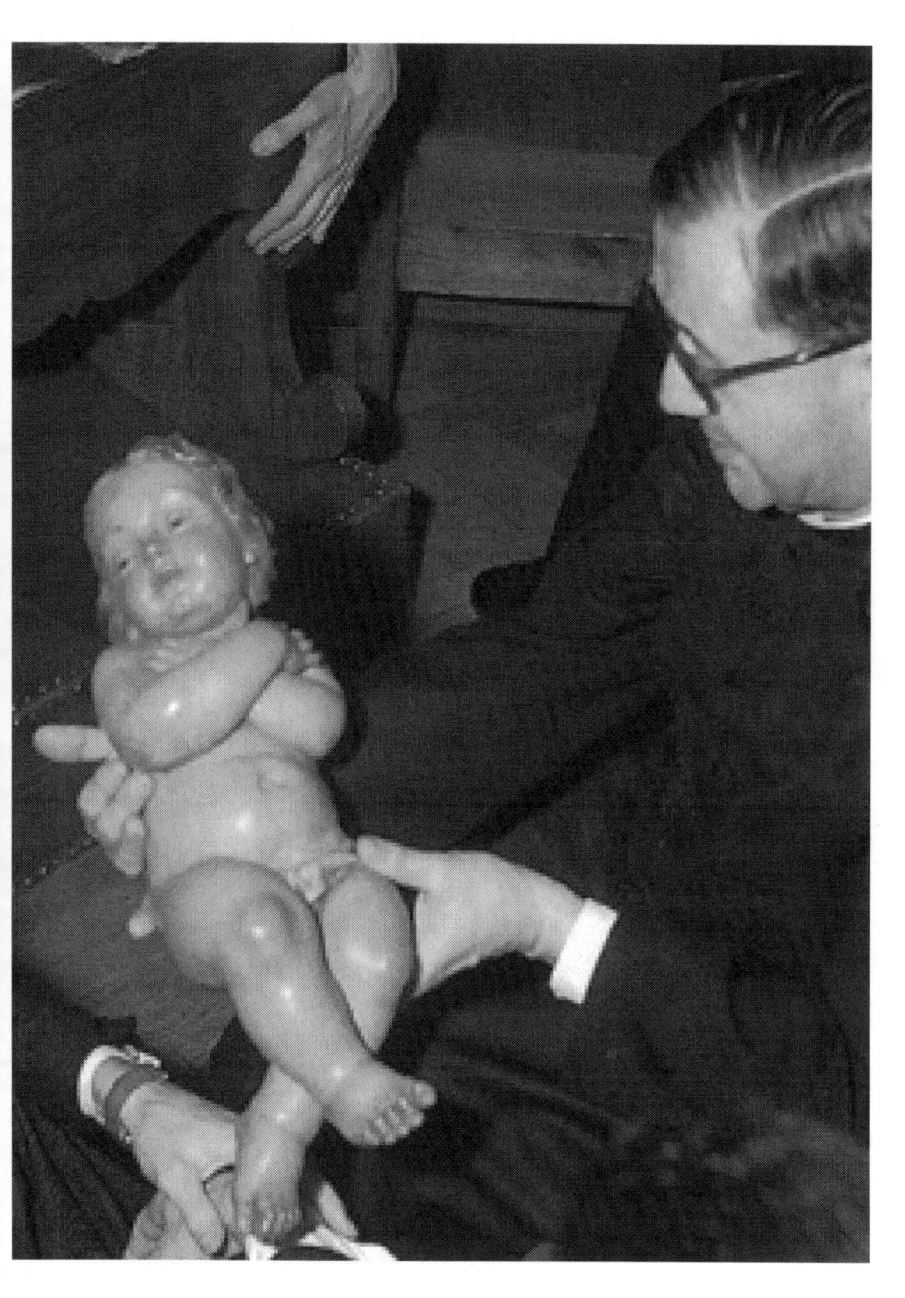

St Josemaría Escrivá adoring the Divine Infant Jesus.

Day Thirty-Six: Redemption.

"He came on earth because omnes homines vult salvos fieri, He wants to redeem the whole world. While you are at your work, shoulder to shoulder with so many others, never forget that there is no soul that does not matter to Christ! Make an effort to spread your Christian spirit to the world about you, so that there may be many friends of the Cross.

-St Josemaría Escrivá

Prayer Intention

Lord Jesus Christ, I humbly ask that You fill me with the spirit of love for all souls in the world, seeing in them the potential for greatness, within this vale of tears. I pray for the grace to see even the lowliest of sinners as most loved and redeemable through You, dear Lord. Wayward souls roam the earth seeking Truth, like orphaned children, in need of a safe place to call their home. It is my duty to lead all souls to the Tabernacle, where You await their arrival, ever merciful, with the promise of everlasting life.

"In Him we have redemption through His blood, the forgiveness of our trespasses, according to the riches of His grace. that He lavished on us with all wisdom and understanding. He made known to us the mystery of His will according to His good pleasure, which He purposed in Christ o usher in the fullness of the times and to bring together in the Messiah all things in heaven and on earth."

- Ephesians 1:7-10

Day Thirty-Six: Redemption.

Dear Lord, I humbly beg You, through the intercession of St Josemaría Escrivá, for the grace to love all souls, for the fidelity and courage to lead all souls to the foot of the Cross, so that they may know of Your love, and forgiveness. Please fill my heart with wisdom to help all sinners become Your faithful servants, like the great St Augustine. Should ninety-nine souls turn their back to you, leaving just one who seeks redemption because of Your graces, may heaven rejoice!

Prayer to St Josemaría Escrivá

Most loving God, through the mediation of Our Lady, the Blessed Virgin, You chose St Josemaría Escrivá to serve You and honour you. You have gifted St Josemaría Escrivá the wisdom and grace to form Opus Dei, a way of sanctification in daily work and in the fulfilment of the Christian's ordinary life and duties. Grant that I too may learn to turn my everyday life into one that serves You God, and imitates the way of St Josemaría Escrivá with a zeal for loving all souls and striving for sanctification. Grant unto me God, through the intercession of St Josemaría Escrivá the favour of (intention).

Day Thirty-Six: Redemption.

"I have been crucified with Christ. It is no longer I who live, but Christ who lives in me. And the life I now live in the flesh I live by faith in the Son of God, who loved me and gave himself for me."

- Galatians 2:20

Holy Rosary of Luminous Mysteries

I believe in God, the Father Almighty, Creator of Heaven, and earth; and in Jesus Christ, His only Son, Our Lord, who was conceived by the Holy Ghost, born of the Virgin Mary, suffered under Pontius Pilate, was crucified; died, and was buried. He descended into Hell; the third day He arose again from the dead; He ascended into Heaven, sitteth at the right hand of God, the Father Almighty; from thence He shall come to judge the living and the dead. I believe in the Holy Spirit, the holy Catholic Church, the communion of saints, the forgiveness of sins, the resurrection of the body, and life everlasting.

Our Father, who art in heaven, hallowed be Thy name; Thy kingdom come; Thy will be done on earth as it is in heaven. Give us this day our daily bread; and forgive us our trespasses as we forgive those who trespass against us; and lead us not into temptation, but deliver us from evil.

Hail Mary, full of grace. The Lord is with thee. Blessed art thou among women, and blessed is the fruit of thy womb, Jesus. Holy Mary, Mother of God, pray for us sinners, now and at the hour of our death.

Glory be to the Father, to the Son, and to the Holy Spirit, as it was, is now, and ever shall be, world without end. Amen.

The Five Luminous Mysteries are prayed on Thursday.

The Luminous Mysteries remind the faithful of Christ's shining light:

The Baptism in the River Jordan (Matthew 3:13–16); The Wedding Feast at Cana (John 2:1–11) The Preaching of the coming of the Kingdom of God (Mark 1:14–15)
The Transfiguration (Matthew 17:1–8); The Institution of the Holy Eucharist (Matthew 26)

Hail Holy Queen

Hail, Holy Queen, Mother of mercy, our life, our sweetness, and our hope. To thee do we cry, poor banished children of Eve, to thee do we send up our sighs, mourning and weeping in this vale of tears. Turn then, most gracious advocate, thine eyes of mercy toward us; and after this our exile show unto us the blessed fruit of thy womb Jesus, O clement, O loving, O sweet Virgin Mary.

Pray for us, O holy Mother of God. That we may be made worthy of the promises of Christ.

O God, whose only begotten Son, by His life, death, and resurrection, has purchased for us the rewards of eternal salvation; grant we beseech Thee, that meditating upon these mysteries of the most holy Rosary of the Blessed Virgin Mary, we may imitate what they contain and obtain what they promise, through the same Christ our Lord.

Prayer to Our Lady of Guadalupe

Our Lady of Guadalupe, Mystical Rose, make intercession for the Holy Church, protect the Sovereign Pontiff, help all those who invoke thee in their necessities, and since thou art the Blessed Virgin Mary, and Mother of the True God, obtain for us from thy most holy Son the grace of keeping our faith, of sweet hope in the midst of the bitterness of life, of burning charity, and the most precious gift of perseverance so that we may carry our cross cheerfully.

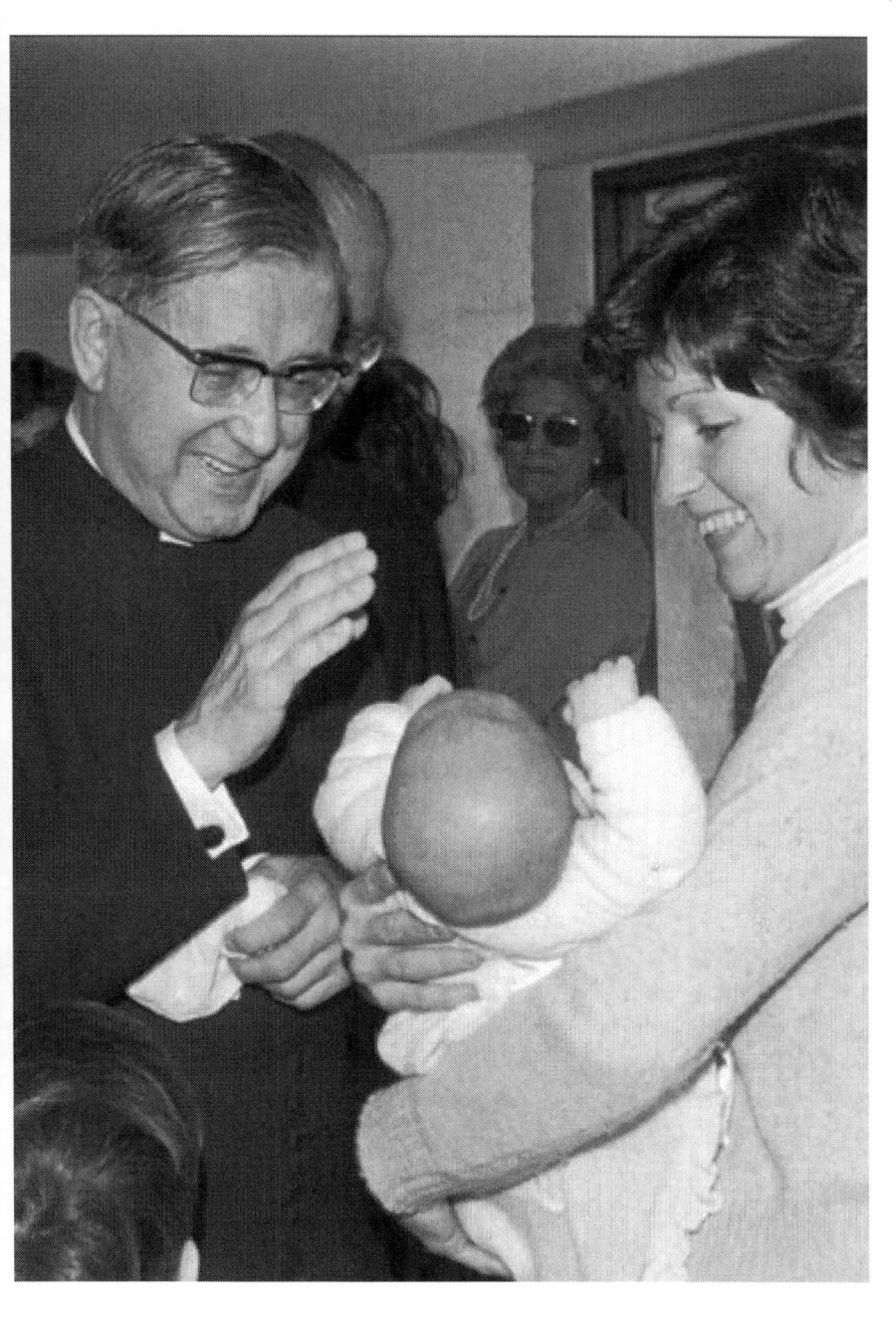

St Josemaría Escrivá blesses members of Opus Dei in Buenos Aires 1974.

Day Thirty-Seven: Instruments of God.

"When God wants to carry out some piece of work, He uses unsuitable means, so that it can be seen that the work is His. How often you have heard me say this! So you and I, who are aware of the massive weight of our failings, should tell Our Lord: "Wretched as I am, I still understand that in your hands I am a divine instrument."

-St Josemaría Escrivá

Prayer Intention

Lord Jesus Christ, I humbly ask that You give me the grace to allow myself each day to be used as an instrument which You, the Grand Conductor, may play in Your heavenly orchestra to fill the ears of the deaf with the melody of Your graces. Like the harp of King David, the ways in which You use me to carry out Your will, play like a beatific song, in which You make Your presence known. I beg of You to use me to carry out the divine mission of the church, so that good fruit may come of it.

"I appeal to you therefore, brothers, by the mercies of God, to present your bodies as a living sacrifice, holy and acceptable to God, which is your spiritual worship. Do not be conformed to this age, but be transformed by the renewing of your mind, so that you may discern what is the good, pleasing, and perfect will of God."

- Romans 12:1-2

Day Thirty-Seven: Instruments of God.

Dear Lord, I humbly beg You, through the intercession of St Josemaría Escrivá, for the grace to humble myself to Thy most holy will. I ask that you make of me an instrument, so that I may always devote myself and my works in all ways which You can use, and are pleasing to You, dear Lord.

Prayer to St Josemaría Escrivá

Most loving God, through the mediation of Our Lady, the Blessed Virgin, You chose St Josemaría Escrivá to serve You and honour you. You have gifted St Josemaría Escrivá the wisdom and grace to form Opus Dei, a way of sanctification in daily work and in the fulfilment of the Christian's ordinary life and duties. Grant that I too may learn to turn my everyday life into one that serves You God, and imitates the way of St Josemaría Escrivá with a zeal for loving all souls and striving for sanctification. Grant unto me God, through the intercession of St Josemaría Escrivá the favour of (intention).

Day Thirty Seven: Instrument of God.

"Whenever the harmful spirit from God was upon Saul, David took the lyre and played it with his hand. So Saul was refreshed and was well, and the harmful spirit departed from him."

- 1 Samuel 16:23

Holy Rosary of Joyful Mysteries

I believe in God, the Father Almighty, Creator of Heaven, and earth; and in Jesus Christ, His only Son, Our Lord, who was conceived by the Holy Ghost, born of the Virgin Mary, suffered under Pontius Pilate, was crucified; died, and was buried. He descended into Hell; the third day He arose again from the dead; He ascended into Heaven, sitteth at the right hand of God, the Father Almighty; from thence He shall come to judge the living and the dead. I believe in the Holy Spirit, the holy Catholic Church, the communion of saints, the forgiveness of sins, the resurrection of the body, and life everlasting.

Our Father, who art in heaven, hallowed be Thy name; Thy kingdom come; Thy will be done on earth as it is in heaven. Give us this day our daily bread; and forgive us our trespasses as we forgive those who trespass against us; and lead us not into temptation, but deliver us from evil.

Hail Mary, full of grace. The Lord is with thee. Blessed art thou among women, and blessed is the fruit of thy womb, Jesus. Holy Mary, Mother of God, pray for us sinners, now and at the hour of our death.

Glory be to the Father, to the Son, and to the Holy Spirit, as it was, is now, and ever shall be, world without end. Amen.

The Five Joyful Mysteries are prayed Monday and Saturday.

The Joyful Mysteries remind the faithful of Our Lady's Fiat and Christ's birth:

The Annunciation (Luke 1:26–38); The Visitation (Luke 1:39–56) The Nativity (Luke 2:1–21); The Presentation (Luke 2:22–38) The Finding of the Child Jesus in the Temple (Luke 2:41–52)

Hail Holy Queen

Hail, Holy Queen, Mother of mercy, our life, our sweetness, and our hope. To thee do we cry, poor banished children of Eve, to thee do we send up our sighs, mourning and weeping in this vale of tears. Turn then, most gracious advocate, thine eyes of mercy toward us; and after this our exile show unto us the blessed fruit of thy womb Jesus, O clement, O loving, O sweet Virgin Mary.

Pray for us, O holy Mother of God. That we may be made worthy of the promises of Christ.

O God, whose only begotten Son, by His life, death, and resurrection, has purchased for us the rewards of eternal salvation; grant we beseech Thee, that meditating upon these mysteries of the most holy Rosary of the Blessed Virgin Mary, we may imitate what they contain and obtain what they promise, through the same Christ our Lord.

Prayer to Our Lady of Guadalupe

Our Lady of Guadalupe, Mystical Rose, make intercession for the Holy Church, protect the Sovereign Pontiff, help all those who invoke thee in their necessities, and since thou art the Blessed Virgin Mary, and Mother of the True God, obtain for us from thy most holy Son the grace of keeping our faith, of sweet hope in the midst of the bitterness of life, of burning charity, and the most precious gift of perseverance so that we may carry our cross cheerfully.

St Josemaría Escrivá in 1975.

Day Thirty-Eight: Unity.

"Pray to God that in the Holy Church, our Mother, the hearts of all may be one heart, as they were in the earliest times of Christianity; so that the words of Scripture may be truly fulfilled until the end of the ages: Multitudinis autem credentium erat cor unum et anima una — the company of the faithful were of one heart and one soul. I am saying this to you in all seriousness: may this holy unity not come to any harm through you. Take it to your prayer!

-St Josemaría Escrivá

Prayer Intention

Lord Jesus Christ, I humbly ask that You give me the grace to unify all Christians through Your most holy Divine Truth, with love and charity. I ask of you Lord, to fill my heart and soul with radiance and warmth, like the midsummer sun which brings the wheat field to fruition so that it may yield a bountiful harvest. Do not allow me to fall to the foul ways of the rat which plagues the grain house, but guide me down the path of the careful farmer who tends to his field with utmost care, for how I tend to Your church will determine if the ripened wheat is sweet, or if it becomes rotted and poisonous from planting seeds of discord.

"Finally, brothers, rejoice. Aim for restoration, comfort one another, agree with one another, live in peace; and the God of love and peace will be with you."

- 2 Corinthians 13:11

Day Thirty-Eight: Unity.

Dear Lord, I humbly beg You, through the intercession of St Josemaría Escrivá, for the grace to sow seeds of harmony and tend to Your church with love and compassion so that we do not become a flock which has scattered among the pastures, but remain strong under your faithful shepherds, whom the wolves flee from.

Prayer to St Josemaría Escrivá

Most loving God, through the mediation of Our Lady, the Blessed Virgin, You chose St Josemaría Escrivá to serve You and honour you. You have gifted St Josemaría Escrivá the wisdom and grace to form Opus Dei, a way of sanctification in daily work and in the fulfilment of the Christian's ordinary life and duties. Grant that I too may learn to turn my everyday life into one that serves You God, and imitates the way of St Josemaría Escrivá with a zeal for loving all souls and striving for sanctification. Grant unto me God, through the intercession of St Josemaría Escrivá the favour of (intention).

Day Thirty-Eight: Unity.

"Now the full number of those who believed were of one heart and soul, and no one said that any of the things that belonged to him was his own, but they had everything in common."

- Acts 4:32

Holy Rosary of Sorrowful Mysteries

I believe in God, the Father Almighty, Creator of Heaven, and earth; and in Jesus Christ, His only Son, Our Lord, who was conceived by the Holy Ghost, born of the Virgin Mary, suffered under Pontius Pilate, was crucified; died, and was buried. He descended into Hell; the third day He arose again from the dead; He ascended into Heaven, sitteth at the right hand of God, the Father Almighty; from thence He shall come to judge the living and the dead. I believe in the Holy Spirit, the holy Catholic Church, the communion of saints, the forgiveness of sins, the resurrection of the body, and life everlasting.

Our Father, who art in heaven, hallowed be Thy name; Thy kingdom come; Thy will be done on earth as it is in heaven. Give us this day our daily bread; and forgive us our trespasses as we forgive those who trespass against us; and lead us not into temptation, but deliver us from evil.

Hail Mary, full of grace. The Lord is with thee. Blessed art thou among women, and blessed is the fruit of thy womb, Jesus. Holy Mary, Mother of God, pray for us sinners, now and at the hour of our death.

Glory be to the Father, to the Son, and to the Holy Spirit, as it was, is now, and ever shall be, world without end. Amen.

The Five Sorrowful Mysteries are prayed Tuesday and Friday.

The Sorrowful Mysteries remind the faithful of Christ's Passion and of His Crucifixion:

The Agony of Jesus in the Garden (Matthew 26:36–56); The Scourging at the Pillar (Matthew 27:26) The Crowning with Thorns (Matthew 27:27–31); The Carrying of the Cross (Matthew 27:32) The Crucifixion (Matthew 27:33–56)

Hail Holy Queen

Hail, Holy Queen, Mother of mercy, our life, our sweetness, and our hope. To thee do we cry, poor banished children of Eve, to thee do we send up our sighs, mourning and weeping in this vale of tears. Turn then, most gracious advocate, thine eyes of mercy toward us; and after this our exile show unto us the blessed fruit of thy womb Jesus, O clement, O loving, O sweet Virgin Mary.

Pray for us, O holy Mother of God. That we may be made worthy of the promises of Christ.

O God, whose only begotten Son, by His life, death, and resurrection, has purchased for us the rewards of eternal salvation; grant we beseech Thee, that meditating upon these mysteries of the most holy Rosary of the Blessed Virgin Mary, we may imitate what they contain and obtain what they promise, through the same Christ our Lord.

Prayer to Our Lady of Guadalupe

Our Lady of Guadalupe, Mystical Rose, make intercession for the Holy Church, protect the Sovereign Pontiff, help all those who invoke thee in their necessities, and since thou art the Blessed Virgin Mary, and Mother of the True God, obtain for us from thy most holy Son the grace of keeping our faith, of sweet hope in the midst of the bitterness of life, of burning charity, and the most precious gift of perseverance so that we may carry our cross cheerfully.

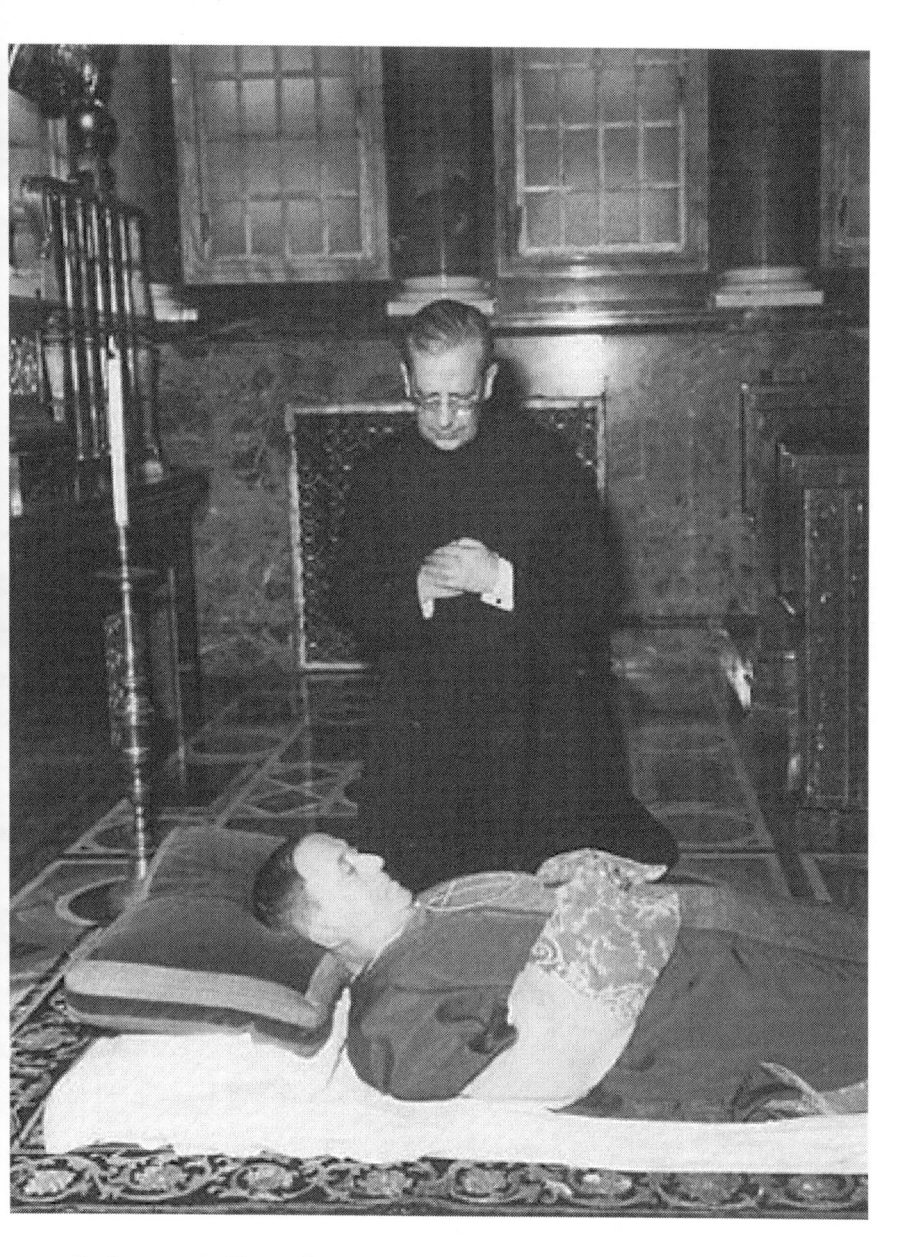

St Josemaría Escrivá rose in glory to heaven, on June 26ᵗʰ, 1975.

Day Thirty-Nine: Reparation.

"There are two reasons, among others, that a friend was saying to himself, why I should make reparation to my Immaculate Mother every Saturday and on the eve of her feasts. On Sundays and on feasts of Our Lady, instead of dedicating such days to prayer, so many people spend them, you have only to look around you and see — offending Our Jesus with public sins and scandalous crimes. Perhaps due to the devil's influence, those of us who want to be good sons are not taking proper care in the way we live these days dedicated to Our Lord and to His Mother. You'll realise that unfortunately these reasons are still very valid. And so, we too should make reparation."

-St Josemaría Escrivá

Prayer Intention

Lord Jesus Christ, I humbly ask that You give me the courage to make reparation for the sins of the world and of mankind who are fallen, including my own sins. I know that through mortification, prayer, attending Mass and partaking in the sacraments that I can grow in my spiritual life so that I may never offend Thee.

"For we must all appear before the judgment seat of Christ, so that each one may receive what is due for what he has done in the body, whether good or evil."

- 2 Corinthians 5:10

Day Thirty-Nine: Reparation.

Dear Lord, I humbly beg You, through the intercession of St Josemaría Escrivá, for the grace and humility to stand before Our Lady, the most humble and compassionate Mother of the world and offer to her my prayers and my sorrows, so that she can take them and give them to You, dear Lord, so that You may transform what very little I have to give, into blessings for those most in need of Your mercy and graces.

Prayer to St Josemaría Escrivá

Most loving God, through the mediation of Our Lady, the Blessed Virgin, You chose St Josemaría Escrivá to serve You and honour you. You have gifted St Josemaría Escrivá the wisdom and grace to form Opus Dei, a way of sanctification in daily work and in the fulfilment of the Christian's ordinary life and duties. Grant that I too may learn to turn my everyday life into one that serves You God, and imitates the way of St Josemaría Escrivá with a zeal for loving all souls and striving for sanctification. Grant unto me God, through the intercession of St Josemaría Escrivá the favour of (intention).

Day Thirty-Nine: Reparation.

"Pay careful attention to yourselves and to all the flock, in which the Holy Spirit has made you overseers, to care for the church of God, which He obtained with His own blood."

- Acts 20:28

Holy Rosary of Glorious Mysteries

I believe in God, the Father Almighty, Creator of Heaven, and earth; and in Jesus Christ, His only Son, Our Lord, who was conceived by the Holy Ghost, born of the Virgin Mary, suffered under Pontius Pilate, was crucified; died, and was buried. He descended into Hell; the third day He arose again from the dead; He ascended into Heaven, sitteth at the right hand of God, the Father Almighty; from thence He shall come to judge the living and the dead. I believe in the Holy Spirit, the holy Catholic Church, the communion of saints, the forgiveness of sins, the resurrection of the body, and life everlasting.

Our Father, who art in heaven, hallowed be Thy name; Thy kingdom come; Thy will be done on earth as it is in heaven. Give us this day our daily bread; and forgive us our trespasses as we forgive those who trespass against us; and lead us not into temptation, but deliver us from evil.

Hail Mary, full of grace. The Lord is with thee. Blessed art thou among women, and blessed is the fruit of thy womb, Jesus. Holy Mary, Mother of God, pray for us sinners, now and at the hour of our death.

Glory be to the Father, to the Son, and to the Holy Spirit, as it was, is now, and ever shall be, world without end. Amen.

The Five Glorious Mysteries are prayed Wednesday and Sunday.

The Glorious Mysteries remind the faithful of Christ's Resurrection and Heaven's glories:

The Resurrection (Luke 24:1-12); The Ascension (Acts 1:6-11) The Descent of the Holy Spirit (Acts 2:1-4); The Assumption (Munificentissimus Deus 44) The Coronation of Mary as Queen of Heaven (Revelations 12:1-6)

Hail Holy Queen

Hail, Holy Queen, Mother of mercy, our life, our sweetness, and our hope. To thee do we cry, poor banished children of Eve, to thee do we send up our sighs, mourning and weeping in this vale of tears. Turn then, most gracious advocate, thine eyes of mercy toward us; and after this our exile show unto us the blessed fruit of thy womb Jesus, O clement, O loving, O sweet Virgin Mary.

Pray for us, O holy Mother of God. That we may be made worthy of the promises of Christ.

O God, whose only begotten Son, by His life, death, and resurrection, has purchased for us the rewards of eternal salvation; grant we beseech Thee, that meditating upon these mysteries of the most holy Rosary of the Blessed Virgin Mary, we may imitate what they contain and obtain what they promise, through the same Christ our Lord.

Prayer to Our Lady of Guadalupe

Our Lady of Guadalupe, Mystical Rose, make intercession for the Holy Church, protect the Sovereign Pontiff, help all those who invoke thee in their necessities, and since thou art the Blessed Virgin Mary, and Mother of the True God, obtain for us from thy most holy Son the grace of keeping our faith, of sweet hope in the midst of the bitterness of life, of burning charity, and the most precious gift of perseverance so that we may carry our cross cheerfully.

St Josemaría Escrivá's shrine and tomb at Our Lady of Peace, Prelatic Church of Opus Dei in Rome.

Day Forty: Jesus Christ.

"We all have to be ipse Christus — Christ himself. This is what Saint Paul commands in the name of God: Induimini Dominum Iesum Christum — put on the Lord Jesus Christ. Each one of us — you! — has to see how he puts on that clothing of which the Apostle speaks. Each one personally, has to sustain an uninterrupted dialogue with the Lord. Jesus is our model. Let us imitate Him. Let us imitate Him by serving the Holy Church and all mankind."

-St Josemaría Escrivá

Prayer Intention

Lord Jesus Christ, I humbly ask that You fill my heart with Your most holy and radiant light so that I may always reflect Your Divine Truth unto the world with the hope of a small child, that it may see the love which you have for all of mankind and grow to love You. Dear sweet Jesus Christ, my Master and most Beloved, who was crucified for the salvation of the world, who rose again and sits at the right hand of the Father in heaven. I will never depart from Thee.

"And Jesus went about all Galilee, teaching in their synagogues, and preaching the gospel of the kingdom, and healing all manner of sickness and all manner of disease among the people. The news spread all over Syria and they brought to Him all those who were sick, stricken with various diseases and pains, dominated by evil spirits, and afflicted with seizures and paralysis, and He healed them."

- Matthew 4:23-24

Day Forty: Jesus Christ.

Dear Lord, I humbly beg You, through the intercession of St Josemaría Escrivá, for the courage to be an example of Your most brilliant and blinding, shining light in this darkened world. You are brighter than all of the stars in the night sky, it is Your light which brings peace among nations and brings satan to his knees, for Your most precious and divine love pierces through the darkness and illuminates the Truth for all to see. Lord, make me an instrument of Your peace.

Prayer to St Josemaría Escrivá

Most loving God, through the mediation of Our Lady, the Blessed Virgin, You chose St Josemaría Escrivá to serve You and honour you. You have gifted St Josemaría Escrivá the wisdom and grace to form Opus Dei, a way of sanctification in daily work and in the fulfilment of the Christian's ordinary life and duties. Grant that I too may learn to turn my everyday life into one that serves You God, and imitates the way of St Josemaría Escrivá with a zeal for loving all souls and striving for sanctification. Grant unto me God, through the intercession of St Josemaría Escrivá the favour of (intention).

Day Forty: Jesus Christ.

"In the same way, let your light shine before others, so that they may see your good works and give glory to your Father who is in heaven."

- Matthew 5:16

Holy Rosary of Luminous Mysteries

I believe in God, the Father Almighty, Creator of Heaven, and earth; and in Jesus Christ, His only Son, Our Lord, who was conceived by the Holy Ghost, born of the Virgin Mary, suffered under Pontius Pilate, was crucified; died, and was buried. He descended into Hell; the third day He arose again from the dead; He ascended into Heaven, sitteth at the right hand of God, the Father Almighty; from thence He shall come to judge the living and the dead. I believe in the Holy Spirit, the holy Catholic Church, the communion of saints, the forgiveness of sins, the resurrection of the body, and life everlasting.

Our Father, who art in heaven, hallowed be Thy name; Thy kingdom come; Thy will be done on earth as it is in heaven. Give us this day our daily bread; and forgive us our trespasses as we forgive those who trespass against us; and lead us not into temptation, but deliver us from evil.

Hail Mary, full of grace. The Lord is with thee. Blessed art thou among women, and blessed is the fruit of thy womb, Jesus. Holy Mary, Mother of God, pray for us sinners, now and at the hour of our death.

Glory be to the Father, to the Son, and to the Holy Spirit, as it was, is now, and ever shall be, world without end. Amen.

The Five Luminous Mysteries are prayed on Thursday.

The Luminous Mysteries remind the faithful of Christ's shining light:

The Baptism in the River Jordan (Matthew 3:13–16); The Wedding Feast at Cana (John 2:1–11) The Preaching of the coming of the Kingdom of God (Mark 1:14–15) The Transfiguration (Matthew 17:1–8); The Institution of the Holy Eucharist (Matthew 26)

Hail Holy Queen

Hail, Holy Queen, Mother of mercy, our life, our sweetness, and our hope. To thee do we cry, poor banished children of Eve, to thee do we send up our sighs, mourning and weeping in this vale of tears. Turn then, most gracious advocate, thine eyes of mercy toward us; and after this our exile show unto us the blessed fruit of thy womb Jesus, O clement, O loving, O sweet Virgin Mary.

Pray for us, O holy Mother of God. That we may be made worthy of the promises of Christ.

O God, whose only begotten Son, by His life, death, and resurrection, has purchased for us the rewards of eternal salvation; grant we beseech Thee, that meditating upon these mysteries of the most holy Rosary of the Blessed Virgin Mary, we may imitate what they contain and obtain what they promise, through the same Christ our Lord.

Prayer to Our Lady of Guadalupe

Our Lady of Guadalupe, Mystical Rose, make intercession for the Holy Church, protect the Sovereign Pontiff, help all those who invoke thee in their necessities, and since thou art the Blessed Virgin Mary, and Mother of the True God, obtain for us from thy most holy Son the grace of keeping our faith, of sweet hope in the midst of the bitterness of life, of burning charity, and the most precious gift of perseverance so that we may carry our cross cheerfully.

St Josemaría Escrivá was Canonised as a saint in heaven by St Pope John Paul II on October 6th 2002.

Preparation for Consecration

Before consecrating yourself to Christ through St Josemaría Escrivá, it is best to attend the sacrament of confession and attend Holy Mass where you can contemplate on Our Lord and His divinity.

Light a candle for Our Lady at the Marian altar and pray for her intercession.

The Salve Regina

English:	Latin:
O, holy Queen, Mother of Mercy, Hail our life, our sweetness and our hope. To thee do we cry, Poor banished children of Eve; To thee do we send up our sighs, Mourning and weeping in this vale of tears. Turn then, most gracious advocate, Thine eyes of mercy toward us;	*Salve, Regina, Mater misericordiæ vita, dulcedo, et spes nostra, salve Ad te clamamus exsules filii Hevæ Ad te suspiramus, gementes et flentes in hac lacrimarum valle.*
And after this our exile, Show unto us the blessed fruit of thy womb, Jesus.	*Eia, ergo, advocata nostra, illos tuos* *misericordes oculos ad nos converte; Et Jesum, benedictum fructum ventris tui, nobis post hoc exsilium ostende.*
O clement, O loving, O sweet Virgin Mary, Pray for us, O holy Mother of God,	*O clemens, O pia, O dulcis Virgo Maria.*
that we may be made worthy of the promises of Christ.	*Ora pro nobis, sancta Dei Genitrix Ut digni efficiamur promissionibus Christi.*

Consecration to Saint Josemaría Escrivá

Consecration Prayer

*Dear Lord Jesus Christ who art in heaven, I_____
come to Thee humbly as an imperfect sinner and humble servant. On
this day, which the sun rose from the east to light the world with
Your warmth and set in the west under the heavens where The
Blessed Virgin, handmaiden of God, shines in the night sky as the
brightest Morning Star; I renew to Thee the solemn vows of my
baptism. I renounce satan, along with all his wicked deeds and pomp.
I proclaim the fullness of the Truth; that Thou Lord Jesus Christ was
crucified and has risen to heaven where Thou sit enthroned at the
right hand of The Father. I believe in the One, Holy and Apostolic
Catholic Church.*

*Out of my own free will and love, I give myself to Thee, Lord Jesus
Christ. I humbly kneel before the choir of Angels, and the Saints of
the heavenly court to consecrate myself to Thee through Thy most
wise and prudent Saint, Josemaría Escrivá de Balaguer y Albás the
Father of Opus Dei. In aeternum te amabo. May all that I have be
given to Thee, and all my deeds be devoted to Thy most holy will.
From this day forward I submit myself fully to Thee, Lord Jesus
Christ, under the guidance and protection of the kindliest father,
servent and Saint, Josemaría Escrivá. May I keep nothing for myself,
so that I may offer every moment of suffering and every moment of
bliss to Thee. For the greater glory of God. Lux mea eris sempiterne.*

Amen.

Hail, Mary, full of grace, the Lord is with thee.
Blessed art thou amongst women
and blessed is the fruit of thy womb, Jesus.
Holy Mary, Mother of God, pray for us sinners,
now and at the hour of our death.
Amen.

References

- *The Way > Scruples > Chap. 10 >* Number 258
- *The Way of the Cross > Eighth Station Jesus consoles the women of Jerusalem >* Number 8
- *Christ is passing by > Finding peace in the Heart of Christ >* Number 166
- *Friends of God > Mother of God and Our Mother >* Number 293
- *Christ is passing by > Marriage: a christian vocation >* Number 22
- *Conversations > Opus Dei: An Association which fosters the Search for Holiness in the World >* Number 62
- *The Way > Heart >* Number 169
- *The Way > Penance >* Number 213
- *Friends of God > Freedom, a gift from God >* Number 30
- *Friends of God > The Christian's Hope > Chap. 13 >* Number 208
- *Christ is passing by > Interior struggle >* Number 76
- *Friends of God > Detachment > Number 115*
- *Christ is passing by > The conversion of the children of God >* Number 64
- *The Way > Poverty >* Number 638
- *The Forge > Struggle >* Number 92
- *Furrow > The Struggle >* Chap. 5 > Number 151
- *The Way > Mortification >* Number 178
- *The Way > Guidance >* Number 77
- *The Forge > Work >* Number 728
- *The Forge > Dazzled >* Chap. 1 > Number 20
- *Friends of God > In the Footsteps of Christ > Chap. 8 > Number 137*
- *Friends of God > Freedom, a gift from God >* Number 32
- *Friends of God > Human Virtues >* Number 89
- *Furrow > Truthfulness > Number 596*
- *Christ is passing by > The Great Unknown >* Number 135
- *Friends of God > Freedom, a gift from God >* Number 38
- *The Forge > Victory >* Number 621

- *Friends of God > The Richness of Ordinary Life > Number 17*
- *Friends of God > Human Virtues >* Number 87
- *Friends of God > Detachment >* Chap. 7
- *Friends of God > Open to God and Men >* Number 174
- *Friends of God > Working for God > Number 62*
- *The Forge > Struggle >* Chap. 2 > Number 131
- *The Forge > Recovery >* Chap. 7 > Number 581
- *The Forge > Recovery >* Chap. 7 > Number 585
- *The Forge > Eternity >* Chap. 13 > Number 991
- *The Forge > Defeat >* Number 191
- *The Forge > Defeat >* Number 192
- *The Forge > To fight once more >* Number 438
- *The Forge > Dazzled >* Number 1
- *The Forge > Victory >* Chap. 8 > Number 646
- *The Forge > Selection >* Number 865
- *The Forge > Fruitfulness >* Number 983
- *The Forge > Victory >* Chap. 8 > Number 610
- *The Forge > Victory >* Number 632
- *The Forge > To fight once more >* Chap. 6 > Number 434
- *The Forge > Struggle >* Number 74